NEW SWAN SHAKESPEARE

GENERAL EDITOR

BERNARD LOTT, M.A., PH.D.

★

Richard II

NEW SWAN SHAKESPEARE

Macbeth

Julius Caesar

Twelfth Night

Richard II

A Midsummer Night's Dream

The Merchant of Venice

Henry V

Romeo and Juliet

Henry IV, Part I

As You Like It

WILLIAM SHAKESPEARE

Richard II

EDITED BY

H. M. HULME, M.A., Ph.D.

LONGMAN

LONGMAN GROUP LIMITED
London

Associated companies, branches and representatives throughout the world

First published 1961
Second impression 1962
New edition (with illustrations) 1967
*New impressions *1969; *1970 (twice); *1972*

ISBN 0 582 52718 X Cased edition
ISBN 0 582 52719 8 Paper edition

Illustrated by John Mousedale

We are indebted to the Local Examinations Syndicate, Cambridge University, for permission to reproduce extracts from the English Literature papers of the Cambridge School Certificate (Overseas), and to the University of London for extracts from the English Literature papers, General Certificate of Education, Ordinary Level.

Printed in Hong Kong by
Dai Nippon Printing co (International) Ltd

INTRODUCTION

The purpose of this book is to give and explain, in the simplest way, the text of one of Shakespeare's plays. The text itself is complete; notes and a glossary have been added to help the reader to understand the play; a section giving hints to examination candidates has been included at the end of the book (page 249). To get the greatest pleasure from it, the reader will need to learn something about the background of the play and its age – and perhaps about Shakespeare himself, for example, or about drama as an art – but his first duty is to understand what the characters are saying and doing, and why they say and do these things.

With this end in view, and to ensure that the help given will in fact simplify the difficulties which are now met with in reading Shakespeare, explanations have been given within the range of a specially-chosen list of 3,000 most commonly used English root-words. Every word in the book which falls outside this list is explained. This is done in the following way:

words which are not used in everyday Modern English as Shakespeare used them, or which are not now used at all, will be found explained in notes on the pages facing the text;

words which are still used in ordinary modern English with their meaning unchanged, but which are not among the 3,000 root-words of the chosen list, will be found explained in the glossary at the back of the book.

References to one or other of these places, and a study of section 3 of this introduction, should be sufficient to remove all difficulty in the understanding of the text. Explanations of longer passages are also given within the range of the word-list.

The rest of this introduction is arranged under the following headings:

1 *The Story of* Richard II

In April 1398, Bolingbroke, an English nobleman, accuses Mowbray of plotting the death of the Duke of Gloucester (uncle of Bolingbroke and of Richard II), who died while a prisoner in Mowbray's charge; it is thought that Richard himself gave orders for Gloucester's death. Because of their quarrel Richard banishes Mowbray for life and Bolingbroke for six years. Soon after Bolingbroke leaves England, his father, old John of Gaunt, dies and King Richard, needing money for his war in Ireland, takes all his possessions. Gaunt's brother, the Duke of York, warns Richard against this injustice, but Richard pays no attention and sails for Ireland, leaving York to rule England in his absence.

Bolingbroke at once returns with an army, declaring that he has come only to claim his inheritance. He wins much support, while York has neither money nor men. Richard comes back too late; landing in Wales, he learns that his Welsh army has scattered, believing their king dead; his favourites have been executed; York and most of the English nobles have joined the all-powerful Bolingbroke. Bolingbroke makes two conditions and Richard has to agree: he will repeal the sentence of banishment and allow Bolingbroke to have his inheritance. As they ride back to London it is clear that Bolingbroke may become king.

Aumerle, York's son, who is still loyal to Richard, is accused of having some part in Gloucester's death. York brings to Parliament Richard's message that he is willing to resign his power, and, as Bolingbroke ascends the throne, one man only, the Bishop of Carlisle, makes a protest. Richard is sent for so that he may, in public, give up his crown to Bolingbroke; Richard's few supporters prepare a plot to kill Bolingbroke.

York discovers his son's part in this and informs Bolingbroke, now King Henry IV. Aumerle is pardoned, but most of the other conspirators are captured and executed. Richard, now a prisoner in a northern castle, is murdered by Exton, but Bolingbroke, who had seemed to wish for Richard's death, refuses to reward his murderer.

2 *The Play as Drama*

Dramatists of Shakespeare's time often based their plays on well-known stories or on actual history and Shakespeare was able to use for *Richard II* the history of his reign as given in Holinshed's *Chronicles of England, Scotland and Ireland* (1577–1586). On this foundation he constructed an exciting and poetic play, adding to and rearranging the things that actually happened, imagining the thoughts and feelings of his characters and writing all their speeches. The play was first printed in 1597, a year or two after its first production.

The theatre in Shakespeare's time was different in some ways from the theatre of today. For example, the stage stretched far out into the open space where the audience sat or stood – so far, in fact, that they were gathered round three sides of it. The fourth side extended back a considerable way, and formed a recess which was roofed over by a second floor. A good deal of action could be set on the upper floor itself; Richard would, no doubt, appear there "on the walls" of Flint Castle (III.iii), and Northumberland would go up to this balcony to give Bolingbroke's message to the king; finally, Richard would come down to the "base court", i.e. to the lower main stage.

This old type of stage was most suitable, too, on the occasions when an actor speaks to himself so as to let the audience know what he is thinking; he would walk to the front of the stage, in close contact with the audience. When Richard is alone in his prison, thinking of his shame, his death and his hope of heaven, he could so express his sorrow and despair that the audience would share his mood and feel, with him, that there was no way out but death.

In the public theatres plays were given in the afternoon, by daylight; as far as is known there was no special stage lighting and practically no scenery. This, as it happens, was to our advantage. For, having no painted scenery, Shakespeare put into the mouths of his characters swift and telling descriptions, poetry which paints the scenes in the mind's eye. We feel the bitter north-east wind as Bolingbroke, about to go into banishment, takes his farewell of Aumerle (I.iv); the scenery of Gloucestershire is brought vividly before us by Northumberland's words (II.iii)

These high wild hills and rough uneven ways . . .

We share the horror of the Welsh captain (II.iv) when

The pale-faced moon looks bloody on the earth.

Things happen more quickly within the play than they could in real life. On the day that Bolingbroke rides away into banishment, Gaunt is suddenly taken ill; Richard hurries to his house and, when Gaunt's death is made known, takes over his possessions; in the same scene Northumberland tells his friends that Bolingbroke, with an army, is returning to England. But as we see or read the play we have no difficulty in accepting this course of events; the speed seems natural.

3 *The Language of the Play*

Shakespeare's language differs in a number of ways from the English we speak today. In this section are listed a number of words, and parts of words, not used today as Shakespeare used them, which occur so often that it would be a waste of space to explain them each time they appeared in the text. These words have either a different meaning from that which we now give them, or are not used in everyday Modern English or are often shortened in Shakespeare's writing to fit in with the metrical pattern of the lines.

adieu – "good-bye".
afore – "before".
alack, alas, exclamations of great sorrow.
an – "if".
aught – "anything".
befall – "happen (to)".
betwixt – "between".
do, does, did are often used with another verb and without adding any separate meaning, e.g. *I do defy him, and I spit at him* (I. i. 60).
e'er – "ever".
ere – "before".
farewell – "good-bye".
flourish – "burst of music".
fond – "foolish".
forthwith – "at once".
'gainst – "against".
hence – "from this place".
hereafter – "after this".
hither – "to this place".
marry – "indeed".
methinks – "it seems to me".
mine – (sometimes) "my".
ne'er – "never".
nor – (sometimes) "neither".
nought – "nothing".
or – (sometimes) "either".
presently – "at once".
quoth – "said".
still – (sometimes) "always".
straight – "at once".

't – "it"; e.g. *will 't* – "will it".
thee – "you" (singular).
thence – "from that place".
thither – "to that place".
thou – "you" (singular).
This is the word often used as the second person singular subject; the verb associated with it ends in *-est* or *-st*, e.g. *what sayst thou to this?* (I.i.110). The verb *to be* and a few others are, however, irregular in this respect, e.g. *Thou art a traitor* (I.i.39). *My life thou shalt command, but not my shame* (I.i.166).
'twixt – "between".
whence – "from which place".
whereupon – "at which".
whither – "to which place".
ye – "you" (plural).
yea – "yes".
yet – (sometimes) "again".
yon, yond – "that, there".

"of" is sometimes shortened to *o'*.

After a plural subject a verb may be found ending in *-s*, as in Northumberland's speech (II.iii.5)

These high wild hills and rough uneven ways
Draws out our miles, and makes them wearisome.

Most of the speeches are in what is called blank verse, i.e. the rhythm depends upon five stressed syllables in each line, the lines being without rhyme:

And fúrbish néw the náme of Jóhn of Gaúnt (I.iii.76).

This kind of verse is very suitable for a play, as the pattern can be easily changed from line to line to fit in with the natural rhythms of speech; the positions of the stressed syllables may vary and the stress may fall lightly on an unaccented syllable:

Howéver Gód or fórtune cást my lót,
There líves or díes, trúe to King Ríchard's thróne,
A lóyal, júst and úpright géntlemán (I.iii.85).

Often as a character is leaving the stage, and very often at the end of a scene, the lines rhyme in a couplet (two lines together):

Cousin, farewell; and uncle, bid him so:
Six years we banish him, and he shall go (I.iii.247).

Where'er I wander, boast of this I can,
Though banished, yet a true born Englishman (I.iii.308).

Rhyme may be used elsewhere to emphasise what a character is saying, e.g. in York's speech (II.i.163)

How long shall I be patient? Oh, how long
Shall tender duty make me suffer wrong?

to draw attention to lines which have the shape and the wisdom of proverbs, e.g. in Gaunt's lines beginning (II.i.7)

Where words are scarce, they are seldom spent in vain,
For they breathe truth that breathe their words in pain,

and to mark a passage of special importance, e.g. Salisbury's news to the king and the king's answer, in the lines beginning (III.ii.71)

Today, today, unhappy day, too late,
O'erthrows thy joys, friends, fortune, and thy state;
For all the Welshmen, hearing thou wert dead,
Are gone to Bolingbroke, dispersed and fled.

An important part of the language of poetry is imagery, which brings an idea of some picture ("image") or perhaps of a sound, a movement, a touch or even a scent, to add to the argument or feeling that is being spoken of. So, for example, Richard addresses Northumberland (V.i.55) as

thou ladder wherewithal
The mounting Bolingbroke ascends my throne.

We know that the king's throne was not so high that Bolingbroke would actually need a ladder to get on to it, but Richard's image reminds us that Northumberland was a most useful instrument for Bolingbroke, bringing him stage by stage, step by step, from claiming his inheritance to claiming the crown itself.

Some very effective similes are found; these are comparisons based on imagery and introduced by such words as *as* or *like*. Northumberland flatters Bolingbroke (II.iii.6),

your fair discourse hath been as sugar.

Salisbury imagines the fall of Richard (II.iv.19),

I see thy glory, like a shooting star,
Fall to the base earth from the firmament.

Imagery takes the form of metaphor when a comparison is not mentioned as such, but suggested, as when Gaunt complains to the king that he will be dead long before his son returns from banishment (I.iii.223),

My inch of taper will be burnt and done,

and when Bolingbroke threatens that, if his inheritance is not restored, he will

lay the summer's dust with showers of blood,
Rained from the wounds of slaughtered Englishmen (III.iii.43).

The kind of image in which a thing or idea is spoken of as a person is known as *personification*. For example, necessity is personified when Richard tells his wife at their parting (V.i.21)

I am sworn brother, sweet,
To grim necessity; and he and I
Will keep a league till death.

An eye is spoke of as a person when the Duchess of York, pleading for her son's life, tells Bolingbroke

Thine eye begins to speak (V.iii.125).

Shakespeare makes his language memorable in other ways than by imagery; he may use *antithesis* (contrast of ideas in neighbouring phrases or sentences of similar structure) as when Bolingbroke says (II.iii.113)

As I was banished, I was banished Hereford,
But as I come, I come for Lancaster.

He may use *paradox* (statement which seems to contradict itself), as when the dying Gaunt rebukes Richard (II.i.91)

Oh no, thou diest, though I the sicker be.

Examples of the *pun* (play on the several meanings of a single word) may be found, as when, to instance the most famous of all, the dying Gaunt plays on the other senses of the word which is his name (II.i.74, 82)

Old Gaunt indeed, and gaunt in being old. . . .
Gaunt am I for the grave, gaunt as a grave. . . . —

Dramatic irony is shown when a speaker understands his words in one way but the audience, or the characters who are listening to him, give more meaning to the speaker's words than he can himself. If we already know from English history that Richard II was deposed, there is a special meaning, which Gaunt and Richard do not know about, in Gaunt's warning description of the king (II.i.108)

Which art possessed now to depose thyself.

And if we are seeing or reading the play for a second time, there is an extra meaning for us in Bolingbroke's words at Coventry (I.iii.48)

For Mowbray and myself are like two men
That vow a long and weary pilgrimage.

We know that both men are to be banished for many years.

4 *The Structure of the Play*

It is generally agreed that *Richard II* is not so perfectly constructed as some of the later plays of Shakespeare; a number of weaknesses can be easily seen. Mowbray, for instance, who at the beginning of the play commands our interest as a powerful opponent of Bolingbroke, leaves the stage after two scenes (I.ii. and I.iii). It is a little strange to have the description of how Bolingbroke and Richard were received as they rode into London (V.ii.1–36) *after* the deposition scene (IV.i) and Richard's parting from his wife (V.i). The question as to whether Aumerle will or will not get his pardon does not perhaps engage our sympathies as much as it should. Sometimes it seems that the action of the play is held up while Richard or one of the other characters makes a long speech of very fine poetry. But we shall find, as we look closely, that the most important part of the play, that part which deals with Bolingbroke's struggle for power, is very well constructed; the energy of Bolingbroke himself seems to bring speed to the events.

The play opens with a strong contrast between the courage and force of character of Bolingbroke and Mowbray and the weakness of a king who tries and fails to end their quarrel. Richard's part in Gloucester's murder, suggested here, is shown more clearly in the next scene. Gaunt accepts that Richard is responsible but takes it for granted also that no subject may take action against his king. We see next the splendour of the lists at Coventry; Bolingbroke hopes to take action against Mowbray. Other faults in Richard's character begin to appear: after allowing all preparations to be made, he stops the fight at the last moment; Mowbray, who has served him, he banishes for life; the sentence on his enemy Bolingbroke he reduces by four years. In the last scene of this first act we look back on the reasons for Richard's jealousy and fear for Bolingbroke; we look forward also to the evil consequences that will follow for the king if he is foolish enough to take Bolingbroke's inheritance.

At the beginning of Act II, Gaunt's rebuke, followed by the protests of the Duke of York, show us why Richard is so unpopular; the nobles are quick to join the returning Bolingbroke. Even the queen, who loves Richard so much, feels that some nameless sorrow is approaching; York is powerless and Richard's favourites expect the worst. Bolingbroke, having returned, gains swift support; his firmness and moderation win York to his side. Richard, by contrast, has not yet come back from Ireland and so his Welsh army is lost to him.

The third act shows the rising power of Bolingbroke and the beginning of Richard's submission; Bushy and Green are executed; Richard discharges his forces. As we see the queen's grief, we have some sympathy with Richard but, as we hear, through the Gardener, the opinions of the ordinary people, we know that he is likely to be deposed.

Act IV brings us to the deposition scene, one of the most important in the play, when Richard gives up his throne to Bolingbroke; in Aumerle and in Carlisle we see some of the opposition to Bolingbroke; the scene ends with a plot against the new king.

Shakespeare now arouses our sympathy for the helpless ex-king; he must part from his queen. York too feels sympathy for Richard but sympathy only; his loyalty as a subject belongs now to Bolingbroke, so that he is ready to denounce his son Aumerle. To Aumerle Bolingbroke can show mercy but the ex-king Richard is to him "a living fear". The visit of the groom reminds us again of the affection which Richard could arouse; his death, now inevitable, comes swiftly. Bolingbroke, just and merciful to Carlisle, mourns the death of Richard which was yet so necessary for his own and England's safety.

5 *The Characters of the Play*

Richard's great mistake is to believe that he is king by divine right (i.e. his power comes from God and his subjects owe him complete obedience); he forgets that he has a duty to rule justly. He spends too much on a splendid court and is too generous to his friends and favourites; as a result he makes himself very unpopular, with nobles and common people alike, through his unjust methods of raising money. He is jealous of Bolingbroke and sympathises with Gaunt's grief only for a moment, when he reduces Bolingbroke's sentence of banishment; for Gaunt's illness he cares little. He lacks judgment and does not realise that the nobles may join solidly against him if he refuses to allow the father to be succeeded by the son.

On his return from Ireland he is full of confidence but empty of power and energy; when he loses confidence he despairs completely. A handsome man, he can call forth love and affection. York, seeing him at Flint Castle, says

> Yet looks he like a king (III.iii.68);

Aumerle remains faithful to him almost until the end. The queen loves him dearly and a poor groom, with great difficulty, gets permission to visit him in prison.

Before his banishment, *Bolingbroke*, as well as Richard, can speak like a poet, but after his return he speaks less about his feelings and concentrates on action. As soon as Richard has set off for Ireland, he lands on the north-east coast, and rides many miles across country to seek out Richard's deputy, the Duke of York. He is very careful to keep public opinion on his side: he persuades York to go with him to Bristol; he gives good reasons for the execution of Bushy and Green; he is most respectful to the king at Flint Castle. His briefest words may have great authority: e.g. to York (III.iii.15)

> Mistake not, uncle, farther than you should;

to Bagot (IV.i.30)

> Bagot, forbear; thou shalt not take it up;

to Northumberland (IV.i.271)

> Urge it no more, my Lord Northumberland.

Even Richard is impressed with the brevity of his comment (IV.i.292)

> The shadow of your sorrow hath destroyed
> The shadow of your face.

Sincerely believing that it is the will of Heaven that he should take the throne, he is careful to gain support wherever he can. He pardons Aumerle and spares the life of Carlisle, but death is the penalty for the others who have plotted against him. He knows that neither England nor himself can be at peace while Richard lives, yet his sorrow at Richard's death is real enough. The play shows that he has many supporters but no friends; his eldest son does not help him at all in the affairs of state.

Gaunt, an old man, who dies shortly after the play begins, is nevertheless a very important character. He believes that Richard is King of England by the will of God, so that, although he thinks that Richard bears some responsibility for the death of Gloucester (Gaunt's brother), he leaves it to God to take vengeance. He is very concerned for the welfare of England and gives his vote for the banishment of Mowbray and Bolingbroke even though this means that he may never see his son again. When he is very near to death he thinks still of England and is ashamed that the king of England should be so much in the power of those who have lent him money. He bitterly rebukes the king for his mismanagement of the state's affairs.

York is wise, honourable and patriotic. He is wise enough to understand that King Richard will not be moved by the words of the dying Gaunt and he tries to keep the peace by excusing the bitterness of Gaunt's rebuke. But when Richard seizes what should be Bolingbroke's inheritance he can be patient no longer, and warns Richard plainly that he will lose the support of the nobles if he does not allow the son to succeed the father. Although Richard pays no attention to his advice he relies on York to rule England in his absence. York has great respect for the law and knows that there is justice in Bolingbroke's claim, but he says very courageously that Bolingbroke is a traitor in returning illegally from banishment, and all who support him are rebels; if he had enough soldiers he would arrest them. As he gradually transfers his loyalty to Bolingbroke, we understand how Bolingbroke wins the support of most of the nation.

York has great personal sympathy for Richard but he believes that England needs a strong and just king. It is he who brings to Bolingbroke the message that Richard is willing to give up the crown and it is he who first hails Bolingbroke as king. To the new king he is completely loyal and he is ready to see his only son Aumerle condemned to death for his part in the plot against Bolingbroke.

Northumberland is a less sympathetic character. He flatters Bolingbroke and takes it for granted that Bolingbroke will become king. York rebukes him for leaving out *King* Richard's title, and he does not kneel to the king at Flint Castle. When he gives Richard the message that Bolingbroke has come only to claim his inheritance, he pretends, on his honour as a gentleman, to believe this. When Richard has given up the crown, Northumberland presses him to read and confess to a list of the offences he has committed while he was king. He urges him four times to do this, showing no pity for Richard's grief and shame. Richard foretells that Northumberland will not be satisfied with the rewards that Bolingbroke gives him and will rebel against him also. This proves true and is part of the story of the later plays of Henry IV.

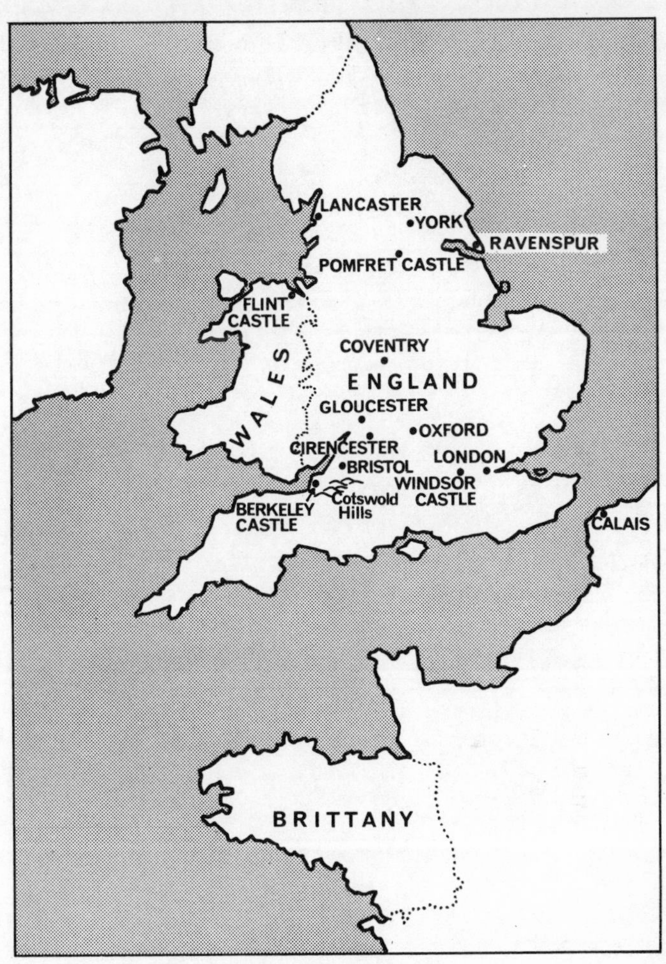

Map showing places named in the play

DRAMATIS PERSONAE

KING RICHARD *the Second*
JOHN OF GAUNT, *Duke of Lancaster* } *uncles of the king*
EDMUND, *Duke of York* }
HENRY, *surnamed* BOLINGBROKE, *Duke of Hereford, son of John of Gaunt; afterwards* KING HENRY IV
DUKE OF AUMERLE, *son of the Duke of York*
THOMAS MOWBRAY, *Duke of Norfolk*
DUKE OF SURREY
EARL OF SALISBURY
LORD BERKELEY
BUSHY }
BAGOT } *servants of King Richard*
GREEN }
EARL OF NORTHUMBERLAND
HENRY PERCY, *called* HOTSPUR, *his son*
LORD ROSS
LORD WILLOUGHBY
LORD FITZWATER
Bishop of Carlisle
Abbot of Westminster
Lord Marshal
SIR STEPHEN SCROOP
SIR PIERCE OF EXTON
Captain of a band of Welshmen
QUEEN *to King Richard*
DUCHESS OF YORK
DUCHESS OF GLOUCESTER
Lady attending on the Queen
Lords, Heralds, Officers, Soldiers, two Gardeners, Keeper, Messenger, Groom, and other Attendants

The scenes are laid in England and Wales.

(I.i) As the play opens we hear that Henry Bolingbroke, Duke of Hereford (then pronounced Harford), has recently made serious accusations against Thomas Mowbray, Duke of Norfolk, and that Bolingbroke's father, John of Gaunt, Duke of Lancaster, has been made responsible for bringing his son before King Richard to repeat his charges. Bolingbroke now accuses Mowbray of high treason and throws down his gauntlet as a challenge to him. Mowbray also is ready to fight to the death to defend his honour. Bolingbroke makes three charges: (1) that Mowbray has kept back, and spent for evil purposes, a large sum of money which was to pay Richard's soldiers, (2) that for the last eighteen years he has been at the centre of every plot made against the state and king, (3) that he plotted the death of the Duke of Gloucester, persuading Gloucester's enemies to murder him. (This Duke of Gloucester was the uncle of Richard and of Bolingbroke; he was a powerful opponent of the king and, as we hear later, Richard was thought by many to have given the orders for his death.) Richard comments coldly on Bolingbroke's excited speech and, in asking Mowbray to reply, promises that, although Bolingbroke is his cousin, both men shall have justice. Mowbray answers: (1) that he spent three-quarters of the money in question for the soldiers in Calais; one quarter he kept, by permission of the king, since Richard owed him money for his expenses in bringing Richard's Queen from France to England, (2) he did not kill Gloucester, but *did* neglect his duty to him, (3) he did once plot to kill Bolingbroke's father but has confessed to this and been pardoned by Gaunt. For the rest, Bolingbroke, he says, is lying, and he is ready to prove this in fighting against him. Richard, after trying, without success, to persuade both men to make up their quarrel, fixes a day for the fight between them.

1 *time-honoured* – "worthy of respect because of your great age".

2 *to make good . . . hear* – "to prove (*make good*) the charge of treason (*appeal*) which he recently (*late*) made so forcefully (*boisterous*) and which then we had not time (*leisure*) to hear and judge . . ." (Richard uses the "royal plural", saying of himself *we* and *our*).

3 *on ancient malice, Or worthily* – "because of some long-standing hatred between them, or deservedly".

4 *As near . . . inveterate malice* – "As far as I was able to examine (*sift*) my son about his reasons (*argument*), he makes the charge because of some dangerous act which it is clear (*apparent*) that Mowbray has planned against (*aimed at*) you, not because of any very old (*inveterate*) enmity" (*sift*, "to pass through a sieve, so separating the truth from what is untrue").

5 *frowning brow to brow* – "one angry (*frowning*) enemy facing another" (*brow*, "forehead").

6 *High-stomached* – "proud".

ACT ONE

Scene I. London. King Richard's palace.

Enter KING RICHARD, JOHN OF GAUNT, *with other* Nobles *and* Attendants.

KING RICHARD

Old John of Gaunt, time-honoured[1] Lancaster,
Hast thou, according to thy oath and bond,
Brought hither Henry Hereford, thy bold son,
Here to make good the boisterous late appeal
Which then our leisure would not let us hear,[2]
Against the Duke of Norfolk, Thomas Mowbray?

GAUNT

I have, my liege.

KING RICHARD

Tell me, moreover, hast thou sounded him
If he appeal the duke on ancient malice,
Or worthily,[3] as a good subject should,
On some known ground of treachery in him.

GAUNT

As near as I could sift him on that argument,
On some apparent danger seen in him,
Aimed at your highness, no inveterate malice.[4]

KING RICHARD

Then call them to our presence; face to face,
And frowning brow to brow,[5] ourselves will hear
The accuser and the accuséd freely speak;
High-stomached[6] are they both, and full of ire,
In rage deaf as the sea, hasty as fire.

7 *Each day . . . your crown* – "May every day add to the happiness of the day before (*other's*), until the gods in heaven, jealous of the good fortune (*hap*) which this world (*earth*) can offer, give you as king a never-dying (*immortal*) fame (*title*)".
8 *but* – "only".
9 *by the cause* – "in the reason for which".
10 *appeal each other of* – "charge each other with".
11 *record* – "witness".
12 *Tendering* – "anxious for".
13 *misbegotten* – "of unworthy origin".
14 *appellant . . . presence* – "making this accusation before the king".
15 *mark . . . well* – "pay great attention to what I call you".
16 *My body . . . in heaven* – "I shall prove true (*make good*) in this world by fighting against you with all my force (*My body*), or else my heavenly soul shall pay (*answer*) for my lies in the next world". Bolingbroke expects to win because he knows he is speaking the truth.
17 *a miscreant . . . clouds* – "an evil-doer (*miscreant*) and just as clouds seem more ugly when the sky is beautiful and full of light (*crystal*), so you deserve death (*too bad to live*) because your actions disgrace your noble birth (*too good to be so*)".
18 *note, With a foul . . . throat* – "disgraceful thing I say, I make you swallow, or accept, the insult of being called an evil (*foul*) and disloyal subject (*traitor*) and you are too choked with guilt to reply".
19 *my right-drawn sword may prove* – "my sword, taken (*drawn*) from its sheath for a just (*right*) reason, may prove to be true (by its victory)".

Enter BOLINGBROKE *and* MOWBRAY

BOLINGBROKE

Many years of happy days befall
My gracious sovereign, my most loving liege!

MOWBRAY

Each day still better other's happiness,
Until the heavens, envying earth's good hap,
Add an immortal title to your crown.[7]

KING RICHARD

We thank you both; yet one but[8] flatters us,
As well appeareth by the cause[9] you come,
Namely, to appeal each other of[10] high treason.
Cousin of Hereford, what dost thou object
Against the Duke of Norfolk, Thomas Mowbray?

BOLINGBROKE

First, heaven be the record[11] to my speech,
In the devotion of a subject's love,
Tendering[12] the precious safety of my prince,
And free from other misbegotten[13] hate,
Come I appellant to this princely presence.[14]
Now, Thomas Mowbray, do I turn to thee,
And mark my greeting well:[15] for what I speak
My body shall make good upon this earth,
Or my divine soul answer it in heaven.[16]
Thou art a traitor and a miscreant,
Too good to be so, and too bad to live,
Since the more fair and crystal is the sky
The uglier seem the clouds[17] that in it fly:
Once more, the more to aggravate the note,
With a foul traitor's name stuff I thy throat,[18]
And wish, so please my sovereign, ere I move,
What my tongue speaks, my right-drawn sword may prove.[19]

20 *Let not my cold words . . . cooled for this* – "Let not my unemotional (*cold*) speech throw doubt on (*accuse*) the energy (*zeal*) with which I defend myself. We cannot decide (*arbitrate*) the quarrel (*cause*) between us two (*twain*) by the angry noise (*bitter clamour*) of sharp (*eager*) talk, testing who is in the right (*trial*) as women do. To decide this (*for this*) the angry (*hot*) blood of one of us must grow cold in death".

21 *fair reverence . . . throat* – "true and proper respect (*fair reverence*) for you as king restrains (*curbs*) me from saying clearly all I wish; otherwise I would hasten (*post*) to accuse Bolingbroke of twice the disloyalty (*treason doubled*) with which he charges me". (*curb*, "to control a horse by pulling on a metal band in its mouth"; *spur*, "a spike on the rider's heel for pricking the horse to make it go faster"; *post*, "to ride fast with a message").

22 *his high blood's royalty* – "the fact that Bolingbroke is of royal family (*blood*)".

23 *let him be . . . liege* – "supposing that he is no relative of my king".

24 *Which to maintain . . . afoot Even* – "and, to support this charge, I would let him have conditions which would favour him (*odds*), and would agree to fight anywhere, even if I were forced (*tied*) to go on foot as far as . . .".

25 *inhabitable* – "not fit to live in".

26 *this* – "this gauntlet (i.e. glove) thrown down as a challenge".

27 *hopes* – "hopes of heaven after my death".

28 *gage* – "pledge". Bolingbroke throws down *his* glove as a sign that he is ready to fight.

29 *Disclaiming here . . . king* – "giving up any claim to be free from attack as a member of the king's family (*kindred*)".

30 *except* – "give as a reason (for not fighting)".

31 *take up . . . pawn* – "pick up my glove, the pledge of my truth".

32 *all the rites . . . else* – "all the other (*else*) rules and ceremonies (*rites*) of knights".

MOWBRAY

Let not my cold words here accuse my zeal:
'T is not the trial of a woman's war,
The bitter clamour of two eager tongues,
Can arbitrate this cause betwixt us twain.
The blood is hot that must be cooled for this.[20]
Yet can I not of such tame patience boast,
As to be hushed and nought at all to say.
First, the fair reverence of your highness curbs me
From giving reins and spurs to my free speech,
Which else would post until it had returned
These terms of treason doubled down his throat.[21]
Setting aside his high blood's royalty,[22]
And let him be no kinsman to my liege,[23]
I do defy him, and I spit at him,
Call him a slanderous coward, and a villain:
Which to maintain, I would allow him odds,
And meet him, were I tied to run afoot
Even[24] to the frozen ridges of the Alps,
Or any other ground inhabitable[25]
Where ever Englishman durst set his foot.
Meantime, let this[26] defend my loyalty!
By all my hopes,[27] most falsely doth he lie!

BOLINGBROKE

Pale trembling coward, there I throw my gage,[28]
Disclaiming here the kindred of the king,[29]
And lay aside my high blood's royalty,
Which fear, not reverence, makes thee to except.[30]
If guilty dread have left thee so much strength
As to take up mine honour's pawn,[31] then stoop.
By that, and all the rites of knighthood else,[32]
Will I make good against thee, arm to arm,
What I have spoke, or thou canst worse devise.

33 *Which gently . . . shoulder* – "with which the king touched my shoulder, as, according to noble custom (*gently*), I knelt before him to be made a knight".
34 *answer thee . . . trial* – "answer your charge in any noble way (*degree*) or knightly fashion (*chivalrous design*) of testing a nobleman's truth (*knightly trial*)".
35 *light* – "alight, get down from my horse".
36 *lay to Mowbray's charge* – "accuse Mowbray of".
37 *great . . . in him* – "something serious if it is to make me have (*inherit*) even a single thought that there is evil in him".
38 *Look what* – "Whatever".
39 *noble*, a gold coin worth 33p., which was then a considerable sum.
40 *In name of lendings for* – "as money given in advance to pay".
41 *detained for lewd employments* – "kept back for his own evil (*lewd*) purposes".
42 *injurious* – "evil".
43 *or elsewhere . . . eye* – "or in any other place, however distant, which Englishmen have seen (*surveyed*)"; (*verge*, "edge").
44 *complotted* – "plotted by men acting together".
45 *Fetch . . . spring* – "have their origin and source in this deceitful Mowbray". (The beginning of a river, where the *spring* of water wells up from the ground, is called its *head*.)
46 *the Duke of Gloucester's death*. Gloucester died in the previous year (1397) while a prisoner at Calais in the charge of Mowbray. Some people believed that he had been murdered on the king's orders. Bolingbroke, in attacking Mowbray, is also attacking King Richard.
47 *Suggest . . . adversaries* – "persuade (*Suggest*) Gloucester's enemies (*adversaries*), who were ready to believe it, that Gloucester was guilty of plotting against King Richard".
48 *like sacrificing Abel's, . . . chastisement*. In a Bible story, a sacrifice made by Abel was pleasing to God, while the sacrifice of Cain, Abel's brother, was not well received. Cain, in anger, killed Abel and God told him that Abel's blood called to him for vengeance. So Gloucester's body, hidden deep in its silent grave (*tongueless cavern*) calls to Bolingbroke for angry (*rough*) punishment (*chastisement*) of his murderers.
49 *glorious worth* – "splendour and nobility".
50 *do it* i.e. punish the murderers of Gloucester.

MOWBRAY

I take it up, and by that sword I swear,
Which gently laid my knighthood on my shoulder,[33]
I 'll answer thee in any fair degree,
Or chivalrous design of knightly trial:[34]
And when I mount, alive may I not light[35]
If I be traitor, or unjustly fight!

KING RICHARD

What doth our cousin lay to Mowbray's charge?[36]
It must be great that can inherit us
So much as of a thought of ill in him.[37]

BOLINGBROKE

Look what[38] I speak, my life shall prove it true:
That Mowbray hath received eight thousand nobles,[39]
In name of lendings for[40] your highness' soldiers,
The which he hath detained for lewd employments,[41]
Like a false traitor and injurious[42] villain.
Besides I say, and will in battle prove,
Or here, or elsewhere to the furthest verge
That ever was surveyed by English eye,[43]
That all the treasons for these eighteen years
Complotted[44] and contrivéd in this land,
Fetch from false Mowbray their first head and spring.[45]
Further I say, and further will maintain
Upon his bad life to make all this good,
That he did plot the Duke of Gloucester's death,[46]
Suggest his soon-believing adversaries,[47]
And consequently, like a traitor coward,
Sluiced out his innocent soul through streams of blood;
Which blood, like sacrificing Abel's, cries,
Even from the tongueless caverns of the earth,
To me for justice, and rough chastisement;[48]
And by the glorious worth[49] of my descent,
This arm shall do it,[50] or this life be spent.

51 *How high . . . soars* – "How great is his determination (*resolution*) – and perhaps also his ambition and pride! Like a bird it seems to fly (*soar*) to a great height (*pitch*)".

52 *bid* – "tell, ask".

53 *slander . . . blood* – "disgrace to his royal family".

54 *Were he* – "if he were".

55 *nay* – "no, even more".

56 *by my sceptre's awe* – "by the fear (*awe*) which my golden rod of office (*sceptre*) inspires . . .".

57 *Such neighbour-nearness . . . soul* – "even that very close relationship (of being brother or heir) to the king would gain Bolingbroke no favour (*privilege*) at all, nor make unfair (*partialise*) the unchanging justice (*firmness*) of my noble mind, which cannot lower itself (*stoop*) to take sides".

58 *as low . . . duly to* – "the words which come from your throat are as untrue as the feelings deep in your heart. Three-quarters of the money I received to use in Calais, I spent (*disbursed*) as was proper (*duly*) on . . .".

59 *For that* – "because".

60 *Upon remainder . . . account* – "for what was left unpaid (*remainder*) of a heavy (*dear*) debt (*account*)".

61 *to fetch his Queen.* Richard's first wife died in 1394 and Mowbray was sent to France in the following year to arrange a marriage between Richard and Isabel, daughter of Charles VI.

62 *swallow down that lie* – "eat your words!" Admit that it is not true that I have wrongly kept money which belongs to the state!

63 *For* – "As for . . .". To this most important charge Mowbray says little: he did not kill Gloucester but he did not properly carry out the duty he had promised.

Now by my sceptre's awe[56]

KING RICHARD

How high a pitch his resolution soars![51]
Thomas of Norfolk, what sayst thou to this?

MOWBRAY

Oh let my sovereign turn away his face,
And bid[52] his ears a little while be deaf,
Till I have told this slander of his blood,[53]
How God and good men hate so foul a liar.

KING RICHARD

Mowbray, impartial are our eyes and ears:
Were he[54] my brother, nay,[55] my kingdom's heir,
As he is but my father's brother's son,
Now by my sceptre's awe,[56] I make a vow,
Such neighbour-nearness to our sacred blood,
Should nothing privilege him, nor partialise
The unstooping firmness of my upright soul.[57]
He is our subject, Mowbray; so art thou.
Free speech and fearless I to thee allow.

MOWBRAY

Then, Bolingbroke, as low as to thy heart,
Through the false passage of thy throat, thou liest!
Three parts of that receipt I had for Calais
Disbursed I duly to[58] his highness' soldiers.
The other part reserved I by consent,
For that[59] my sovereign liege was in my debt,
Upon remainder of a dear account,[60]
Since last I went to France to fetch his Queen:[61]
Now swallow down that lie![62] For[63] Gloucester's death,
I slew him not; but, to my own disgrace,
Neglected my sworn duty in that case.
For you, my noble Lord of Lancaster,

64 *A trespass . . . vex* – "a sin (*trespass*) which troubles (*vex*) . . .".
65 *exactly* – "very properly, as I should".
66 *my fault* – "what I am guilty of".
67 *appealed, It issues* – "with which I am charged, it comes from, has its origin in . . .".
68 *recreant* – "cowardly".
69 *Which in myself . . . defend* – "and I will boldly defend myself in person".
70 *interchangeably* – "in exchange (for Bolingbroke's pledge)".
71 *overweening* – "too proud".
72 *in the best blood . . . whereof* – "by shedding that blood, royal (*best*) but disgraced, which lies near his heart: and so that I may do this quickly . . .".
73 *Wrath-kindled* – "Set on fire (*kindled*) with anger (*wrath*)".
74 *Let 's purge . . . incision* – "Let us agree to clear from your bodies (*purge*) this hot-tempered bile (*choler*), without opening a vein to let out blood (a method believed to cure illness in earlier times). Although I am no doctor (*physician*), I order (*prescribe*) this medicine. Deep-rooted hatred makes cuts (*incision*) which go too deep".
75 *conclude, and be agreed* – "end your dispute and be friends".
76 *no month to bleed* – "not a good time to cure by blood-letting".
77 *make-peace* – "peace-maker".

Throw down, my son, the Duke of Norfolk's gage

The honourable father to my foe,
Once did I lay an ambush for your life,
A trespass that doth vex[64] my grievéd soul;
But, ere I last received the sacrament,
I did confess it, and exactly[65] begged
Your grace's pardon, and I hope I had it.
This is my fault.[66] As for the rest appealed,
It issues[67] from the rancour of a villain,
A recreant[68] and most degenerate traitor;
Which in myself I boldly will defend,[69]
And interchangeably[70] hurl down my gage
Upon this overweening[71] traitor's foot,
To prove myself a loyal gentleman
Even in the best blood chambered in his bosom:
In haste whereof,[72] most heartily I pray
Your highness to assign our trial day.

KING RICHARD

Wrath-kindled[73] gentlemen, be ruled by me:
Let 's purge this choler without letting blood!
This we prescribe, though no physician:
Deep malice makes too deep incision.[74]
Forget, forgive; conclude, and be agreed,[75]
Our doctors say this is no month to bleed.[76]
Good uncle, let this end where it begun;
We 'll calm the Duke of Norfolk; you, your son.

GAUNT

To be a make-peace[77] shall become my age:
Throw down, my son, the Duke of Norfolk's gage.

KING RICHARD

And, Norfolk, thrown down his.

78 *When ... again* – "When will you do what I ask? The obedience you owe me tells you that I should not ask you twice."

79 *no boot* – "no remedy, no alternative".

80 *dread* – "feared".

81 *thou shalt command* – "you have the right to ask for".

82 *my fair name ... have* – "my unstained reputation that, in spite of death, will live upon my grave, you shall not command to the service (*use*) of shameful dishonour".

83 *impeached, and baffled* – "charged with treason, and disgraced as a knight".

84 *Pierced to the soul ... poison* – "stabbed to the heart by Bolingbroke's poisoned (*venomed*) untrue reports (*slander*), and no ointment (*balm*) can help me except (*but*) blood from the heart of the one who spoke (*breathed*) these words of poison".

85 *Give me ... tame.* Richard commands Mowbray to give him Bolingbroke's glove. Nobles, however courageous, must obey their king, even as a lion, king of beasts, can subdue (*make tame*) the fierce leopard. (A golden leopard was the sign on Mowbray's family shield; lions are painted on the shield of the English kings.)

86 *but not change his spots ... gage* – "even a king cannot change a man's character. I would give up (*resign*) his glove at your command, if only (*but*) you could take also the disgrace (*shame*) I should feel in not accepting his challenge to fight". (We still use the proverb "The leopard cannot change his spots", meaning that character cannot be altered.)

87 *mortal times afford* – "that our human life can offer".

88 *that away ... loam* – "without that, men are like nothing more than (*but*) gold-coloured (*gilded*) earth". (Their claim to be thought noble is only a fine pretence.)

89 *ten times barred-up chest* – "a box fastened (against thieves) ten times over". A noble heart in a man's chest is like a jewel in a safe box. Mowbray is playing on the two meanings of the word *chest.*

90 *in one* – "from one root, on one stem".

Lions make leopards tame[85]

GAUNT

When, Harry, when?
Obedience bids I should not bid again.[78]

KING RICHARD

Norfolk, throw down, we bid; there is no boot.[79]

MOWBRAY

Myself I throw, dread[80] sovereign, at thy foot.
My life thou shalt command,[81] but not my shame,
The one my duty owes, but my fair name,
Despite of death that lives upon my grave,
To dark dishonour's use thou shalt not have.[82]
I am disgraced, impeached, and baffled[83] here,
Pierced to the soul with slander's venomed spear,
The which no balm can cure but his heart-blood
Which breathed this poison.[84]

KING RICHARD

Rage must be withstood:
Give me his gage! Lions make leopards tame.[85]

MOWBRAY

Yea, but not change his spots. Take but my shame,
And I resign my gage.[86] My dear, dear lord,
The purest treasure mortal times afford[87]
Is spotless reputation: that away,
Men are but gilded loam[88] or painted clay.
A jewel in a ten times barred-up chest[89]
Is a bold spirit in a loyal breast.
Mine honour is my life; both grow in one:[90]
Take honour from me, and my life is done.

91 *try* – "put to the test".
92 *throw up* – "give up", i.e. throw the gauntlet to the ground again.
93 *crest-fallen* – "humbled, letting fall the tuft of feathers (*crest*) on my helmet".
94 *with pale . . . dastard* – "by looking pale with fear as a beggar might, make Mowbray's accusation seem true (*impeach*) and lower my high rank (*height*) in the eyes of (*before*) this coward whom I have challenged (*out-dared*)?"
95 *sound so base a parle* – "ask in so cowardly a way (*so base*) that there shall be no fight"; (*sound a parle*, to blow a note on a trumpet asking for a truce).
96 *tear . . . fear* – "tear out my tongue, the slave-like instrument (*motive*) of a fear that takes back the words it has spoken earlier (*recanting*)".
97 *in his high disgrace* – "to his great dishonour".
98 *harbour* – "have its home".
99 *sue* – "beg".
100 *Which since . . . do* – "And since I cannot make you obey my command . . .".
101 *as your lives . . . it* – "on penalty of death, if you disobey".
102 *Saint Lambert's day*. September 17.
103 *arbitrate . . . hate* – "decide (*arbitrate*) the angry (*swelling*) quarrel (*difference*) of your unchangeable (*settled*) hatred for each other".
104 *atone you* – "make you friends again".
105 *see Justice . . . chivalry* – "see the contest between you and see how the justice of heaven will show (*design*) the true nobility (*chivalry*) of the one who wins (*victor's*)". The knight who wins the contest will be the one who spoke the truth.
106 *officers at arms . . . alarms* – "officers who arrange these combats to make all preparations for this fight between two Englishmen (*home alarms*)".

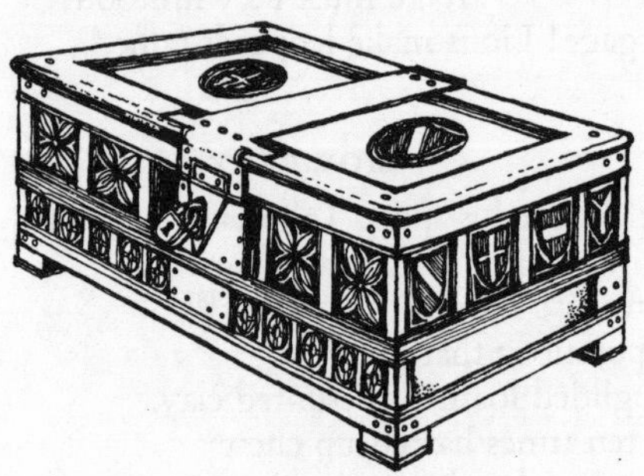

A jewel in a ten times barred-up chest[89]

Then, dear my liege, mine honour let me try;[91]
In that I live; and for that will I die.

KING RICHARD

Cousin, throw up[92] your gage; do you begin!

BOLINGBROKE

Oh, God defend my soul from such deep sin!
Shall I seem crest-fallen[93] in my father's sight,
Or with pale beggar-fear impeach my height
Before this out-dared dastard?[94] Ere my tongue
Shall wound my honour with such feeble wrong,
Or sound so base a parle,[95] my teeth shall tear
The slavish motive of recanting fear,[96]
And spit it bleeding in his high disgrace,[97]
Where shame doth harbour,[98] even in Mowbray's face.

KING RICHARD

We were not born to sue,[99] but to command;
Which since we cannot do[100] to make you friends,
Be ready, as your lives shall answer it,[101]
At Coventry, upon Saint Lambert's day:[102]
There shall your swords and lances arbitrate
The swelling difference of your settled hate:[103]
Since we cannot atone you,[104] we shall see
Justice design the victor's chivalry.[105]
Lord Marshal, command our officers at arms,
Be ready to direct these home alarms.[106]

[*Exeunt*

(I.ii) The Duchess of Gloucester, widow of the Duke, has asked her brother-in-law, John of Gaunt, to help her to revenge her husband's murder. Gaunt answers that he would like to see those who have killed his brother Woodstock receive their punishment, but it is King Richard who must punish them; if he will not, they must trust that God will take revenge. It is the king who has caused Gloucester's death, and, if the king's action was wrong, God must revenge it. The duchess hopes that Mowbray will be killed by Bolingbroke.

1 *the part . . . stir* – "the fact that I was Gloucester's (*Woodstock's*) brother calls (*solicit*) me, even more than your exclamations (*exclaims*) of sorrow, to take action (*stir*) . . .".

2 *correction . . . heads* – "the power to punish (*correction*) is in the hands of that man – the king – who himself did the wrong which we, as subjects, cannot punish, let us entrust (*Put we*) to God the punishment we think should be (*our quarrel*). When God sees that the time (*hours*) is ready (*ripe*), he will send down evil in return for evil (*vengeance*), which will fall like hot rain on the heads of the guilty".

3 *Finds brotherhood . . . spur* – "Does not the fact that you were Gloucester's brother drive you on faster to revenge?" (*Spur*, "a sharp point fixed to the heel of a rider for pricking a horse to make it go faster".)

4 *Some of those seven . . . cut* – "Of these seven sons of Edward III, holy containers (*vials*) of his blood, branches of his family tree, four have died natural deaths of age or illness (*by nature's course*); their blood has dried up; fate (*the destinies*) has cut down those branches".

5 *the precious liquor*. The holy blood and the sap of the tree.

6 *his summer leaves all faded*. Gloucester was put to death just when he was at the best part of his life. (He was born in 1355 and died in 1397.)

7 *envy's hand* – "by the hand of an enemy"; (*envy*, "enmity").

8 *That metal . . . a man* – "You and he were born of the same father and mother, as if the liquid metal that makes a man was poured into the same (*self*) mould".

9 *art thou slain . . . life* – "some part of you has been murdered in his murder. You agree (*consent*) in part to your father's death when you look on, and take no action (*seest*), while your brother, a copy (*model*) of your father, is miserably (*wretched*) killed".

Scene II. The Duke of Lancaster's palace.

Enter JOHN OF GAUNT *and the* DUCHESS OF GLOUCESTER.

GAUNT

Alas, the part I had in Woodstock's blood
Doth more solicit me than your exclaims,
To stir[1] against the butchers of his life!
But since correction lieth in those hands
Which made the fault that we cannot correct,
Put we our quarrel to the will of heaven,
Who, when they see the hours ripe on earth,
Will rain hot vengeance on offenders' heads.[2]

DUCHESS

Finds brotherhood in thee no sharper spur?[3]
Hath love in thy old blood no living fire?
Edward's seven sons, whereof thyself art one,
Were as seven vials of his sacred blood,
Or seven fair branches springing from one root.
Some of those seven are dried by nature's course,
Some of those branches by the destinies cut:[4]
But Thomas, my dear lord, my life, my Gloucester
One vial full of Edward's sacred blood,
One flourishing branch of his most royal root
Is cracked, and all the precious liquor[5] spilt;
Is hacked down, and his summer leaves all faded[6]
By envy's hand,[7] and murder's bloody axe.
Ah, Gaunt! His blood was thine! That bed, that womb,
That metal, that self-mould that fashioned thee
Made him a man:[8] and though thou liv'st and breath'st,
Yet art thou slain in him. Thou dost consent
In some large measure to thy father's death,
In that thou seest thy wretched brother die,
Who was the model of thy father's life.[9]

10 *In suffering . . . thy life* – "in allowing (*suffering*) your brother to be killed in this way (*thus*), you leave the way open (*naked*) for your own death".

11 *mean men* – "men who are not of noble family".

12 *venge* – "take revenge for".

13 *Where then . . . myself?* – "To whom, if you will not help me, can I complain?"

14 *behold* – "see".

15 *fell* – "dangerous".

16 *sit my husband's wrongs . . . my cousin Hereford* – "may the injuries (*wrongs*) done to my husband rest on Bolingbroke's spear and guide that spear to wound Gloucester's murderer. Or, if this evil happening (*misfortune*) does not strike Mowbray down (*miss*) at their first onrush (*career*), may the load of his guilt be so heavy in his heart that it breaks the spine of his energetic horse (*courser*), so that the rider, Mowbray, is thrown head first (*headlong*) to the ground, inside the enclosure where they fight (*lists*), and is recognised as a coward (*caitiff*) conquered by (*recreant to*) my relative (*cousin*) Bolingbroke".

17 *sometimes* – "former".

Call it not patience, Gaunt; it is despair;
In suffering thus thy brother to be slaughtered,
Thou showest the naked pathway to thy life,[10]
Teaching stern murder how to butcher thee.
That which, in mean men,[11] we entitled patience
Is pale cold cowardice in noble breasts:
What shall I say? To safeguard thine own life,
The best way is to venge[12] my Gloucester's death.

GAUNT

God's is the quarrel; for God's substitute,
His deputy anointed in His sight,
Hath caused his death; the which, if wrongfully,
Let heaven revenge; for I may never lift
An angry arm against his minister.

DUCHESS

Where then, alas, may I complain myself?[13]

GAUNT

To God, the widow's champion and defence.

DUCHESS

Why, then, I will! Farewell, old Gaunt.
Thou goest to Coventry, there to behold[14]
Our cousin Hereford and fell[15] Mowbray fight.
Oh, sit my husband s wrongs on Hereford's spear,
That it may enter butcher Mowbray's breast!
Or, if misfortune miss the first career,
Be Mowbray's sins so heavy in his bosom
That they may break his foaming courser's back,
And throw the rider headlong in the lists,
A caitiff recreant to my cousin Hereford![16]
Farewell, old Gaunt! Thy sometimes[17] brother's wife
With her companion, grief, must end her life.

18 *good stay* – "good fortune remain . . .".

19 *Grief boundeth . . . begun* – "Sorrow (*Grief*) which is heavy and which has good reason (*weight*) is like a bouncing ball which jumps up and down (*boundeth*) – and cannot be still and silent – in the person whom it strikes (*where it falls*); only the person whose grief is not sincere (*empty hollowness*) can stop complaining. I am saying good-bye too early, when I have hardly begun to speak of my sorrow".

20 *done* – "finished".

21 *Commend me* – "Give my greetings . . .".

22 *empty lodgings . . . stones* – "empty rooms (*lodgings*), walls without their tapestries (*unfurnished*), kitchen quarters (*offices*) without servants in them, floors on which no one walks". Plashy was the country home of Gloucester and his wife.

23 *dwells* – "lives, is found".

(I.iii) At Coventry, Bolingbroke, Duke of Hereford, and Mowbray, Duke of Norfolk, are ready to enter the enclosure in which they are to fight. The king and his nobles take their places; Mowbray who is to defend himself, and Bolingbroke who makes the accusation against him, say good-bye to the king and to their friends; one of them is now to die. But just as the fight is to begin, King Richard stops it and makes known what he and his council of nobles have decided: to keep England at peace, Bolingbroke is ordered to leave England for ten years, Mowbray is banished for ever. They are asked to swear that they will not meet and join together in any plot against king or state. Mowbray leaves but, because of the sorrow of John of Gaunt, Richard reduces the sentence of Bolingbroke by four years. Gaunt fears he will not live to see his son again. He tries to comfort Bolingbroke.

1 *lists* – "enclosure in which the contest was to take place".

2 *armed* – "ready, in his armour".

3 *at all points . . . in* – "in every detail, and is eager to come into the lists".

GAUNT

Sister, farewell: I must to Coventry!
As much good stay[18] with thee as go with me!

DUCHESS

Yet one word more! Grief boundeth where it falls,
Not with the empty hollowness, but weight.
I take my leave before I have begun,[19]
For sorrow ends not when it seemeth done.[20]
Commend me[21] to thy brother, Edmund York.
Lo, this is all – nay, yet depart not so –
Though this be all, do not so quickly go;
I shall remember more. Bid him – ah, what?
With all good speed at Plashy visit me.
Alack, and what shall good old York there see
But empty lodgings, and unfurnished walls,
Unpeopled offices, untrodden stones?[22]
And what hear there for welcome, but my groans?
Therefore commend me; let him not come there
To seek out sorrow that dwells[23] every where:
Desolate, desolate will I hence, and die;
The last leave of thee takes my weeping eye.

[*Exeunt*

Scene III. The lists[1] *at Coventry*

Enter the Lord Marshal *and the* DUKE OF AUMERLE.

MARSHAL

My Lord Aumerle, is Harry Hereford armed?[2]

AUMERLE

Yea, at all points, and longs to enter in.[3]

4 *sprightfully and bold . . . trumpet* – "active (*sprightfully*) and brave, is only (*but*) waiting for (*stays*) the trumpet of the knight who is making the accusation (*appellant*)".
5 *champions* – "knights who are to fight for their honour".
6 *set* – "seated in their places".
7 *defendant* – "the knight who is defending himself against the accusation".
8 *orderly proceed . . . cause* – "go on (*proceed*) according to the rules of tournaments (*orderly*) to make him swear that (*swear him in*) he is fighting for a true reason".
9 *knightly clad in arms* – "dressed (*clad*) in the armour of a knight".
10 *As so . . . valour* – "and, as you speak the truth, so may God and your courage (*valour*) keep you safe".
11 *engagéd* – "as I have promised".
12 *Which God . . . violate* – "and God forbid (*defend*) that a knight should break (*violate*) his oath".
13 *my succeeding issue* – "my children (*issue*) who will come after me (*succeeding*)".
14 *appeals* – "accuses and challenges".
15 *truly* – "with truth on my side".

MARSHAL

The Duke of Norfolk, sprightfully and bold,
Stays but the summons of the appellant's trumpet.[4]

AUMERLE

Why then, the champions[5] are prepared, and stay
For nothing but his majesty's approach.

The trumpets sound, and the KING *enters with his nobles,* GAUNT, BUSHY, BAGOT, GREEN, *and others: when they are set,*[6] *enter* MOWBRAY *in arms, defendant,*[7] *with a* Herald.

KING RICHARD

Marshal, demand of yonder champion
The cause of his arrival here in arms;
Ask him his name, and orderly proceed
To swear him in the justice of his cause.[8]

MARSHAL

In God's name, and the king's, say who thou art,
And why thou com'st thus knightly clad in arms,[9]
Against what man thou com'st, and what thy quarrel;
Speak truly, on thy knighthood and thy oath,
As so defend thee heaven and thy valour.[10]

MOWBRAY

My name is Thomas Mowbray, Duke of Norfolk,
Who hither come engagéd[11] by my oath –
Which God defend a knight should violate –[12]
Both to defend my loyalty and truth,
To God, my king, and my succeeding issue,[13]
Against the Duke of Hereford that appeals[14] me;
And by the grace of God, and this mine arm,
To prove him, in defending of myself,
A traitor to my God, my king, and me,
And as I truly[15] fight, defend me heaven!

16 *appellant* – "the knight who makes the charge".

17 *plated in habiliments of war* – "in plated armour"; (*plated*, "covered with sheets of metal"; *habiliments*, "equipment, dress").

18 *Depose him in* – "ask him to say on oath . . ."

19 *pain* – "penalty".

20 *daring-hardy . . . lists* – "foolishly brave as to touch anything inside the tournament enclosure".

21 *direct these fair designs* – "be in charge of (*direct*) these splendid (*fair*) preparations (*designs*)".

Thus plated in habiliments of war[17]

The trumpets sound. Enter BOLINGBROKE, *appellant,*[16] *in armour, with a* Herald.

KING RICHARD

Marshal, ask yonder knight in arms,
Both who he is, and why he cometh hither
Thus plated in habiliments of war:[17]
And formally, according to our law,
Depose him in[18] the justice of his cause.

MARSHAL

What is thy name and wherfore com'st thou hither
Before King Richard in his royal lists?
Against whom com'st thou and what 's thy quarrel?
Speak like a true knight, so defend thee heaven!

BOLINGBROKE

Harry of Hereford, Lancaster, and Derby
Am I: who ready here do stand in arms,
To prove by God's grace, and my body's valour,
In lists, on Thomas Mowbray, Duke of Norfolk,
That he 's a traitor, foul and dangerous,
To God of heaven, King Richard, and to me,
And as I truly fight, defend me heaven!

MARSHAL

On pain[19] of death, no person be so bold
Or daring-hardy as to touch the lists,[20]
Except the Marshal, and such officers
Appointed to direct these fair designs.[21]

BOLINGBROKE

Lord Marshal, let me kiss my sovereign's hand,
And bow my knee before his majesty:
For Mowbray and myself are like two men

22 *vow . . . pilgrimage.* One of them may expect to die and so go on a long journey, not to a holy place on this earth, but to the holy world beyond the grave. In fact, as we shall see, they are both to go into exile.

23 *take a ceremonious leave . . . friends,* "say good-bye solemnly and formally and receive in parting the good wishes of the friends of each of us".

24 *in all duty* – "with all the loyalty of a subject".

25 *descend and fold him* – "come down (from the balcony over the back of the stage) and take him close . . ."

26 *as thy cause . . . fortune* – "if what you are fighting for (*thy cause*) is true, may you have success (*fortune*) . . .".

27 *my blood . . . dead* – "as my cousin, you have my blood in your veins, but if, losing the fight, you let fall (*shed*) some of this blood (*which*), I can, as king, feel sorry for (*lament*) your death, but not take revenge against Mowbray".

28 *let no noble . . . tear* – "it would not be right (*profane*) for the eye of any man of noble nature to let fall a tear" (*profane,* "put to evil use").

29 *falcon,* a bird trained to hunt other birds, quick and certain.

30 *sick* – "ill".

31 *cheerly* – "cheerfully".

32 *regreet* – "salute, come to". (Sweets were served at the end of dinner. Bolingbroke greets last of all the one he loves best.)

33 *author* – "father".

34 *Whose youthful . . . regenerate.* The courage (*spirit*) which his father had when he was young (*youthful*) has been born again (*regenerate*) in his son.

35 *proof* – "strength against an enemy's blows".

36 *steel* – "make strong as steel".

37 *waxen coat* – "armour which will be as soft as wax".

38 *furbish new* – "bring new polish (new fame) to . . ."

39 *lusty 'haviour* – "brave conduct (*'haviour,* "behaviour") of someone young and strong (*lusty*)".

That vow a long and weary pilgrimage;[22]
Then let us take a ceremonious leave
And loving farewell of our several friends.[23]

MARSHAL

The appellant in all duty[24] greets your highness,
And craves to kiss your hand and take his leave.

KING RICHARD

We will descend and fold him[25] in our arms.
Cousin of Hereford, as thy cause is right,
So be thy fortune[26] in this royal fight!
Farewell, my blood, which if today thou shed,
Lament we may, but not revenge thee dead.[27]

BOLINGBROKE

Oh, let no noble eye profane a tear[28]
For me, if I be gored with Mowbray's spear!
As confident as is the falcon's[29] flight
Against a bird, do I with Mowbray fight.
[*to the* Marshal] My loving lord, I take my leave of you,
Of you, my noble cousin, Lord Aumerle;
Not sick,[30] although I have to do with death,
But lusty, young, and cheerly[31] drawing breath.
Lo, as at English feasts, so I regreet[32]
The daintiest last, to make the end most sweet;
[*to* GAUNT] Oh thou, the earthly author[33] of my blood,
Whose youthful spirit, in me regenerate,[34]
Doth with a twofold vigour lift me up
To reach at victory above my head,
Add proof[35] unto mine armour with thy prayers,
And with thy blessings steel[36] my lance's point,
That it may enter Mowbray's waxen coat,[37]
And furbish new[38] the name of John of Gaunt,
Even in the lusty 'haviour[39] of his son.

40 *prosperous* – "successful".
41 *swift . . . execution* – "quick (*swift*) as lightning flashes in carrying out (*execution*) what you have decided".
42 *like amazing thunder . . . enemy* – "like the noise of thunder, stunning (*amazing*) and deafening, on the helmet (*casque*) of your dangerous (*adverse*) and wicked (*pernicious*) foe".
43 *Mine innocence . . . thrive!* – "I ask that I may ucceed (*thrive*) because of my innocence and by the help of St. George of England!"
44 *cast my lot* – "decide my fate".
45 *Never did captive . . . battle* – "No prisoner (*captive*) has ever more gladly (*with a freer heart*) thrown (*cast*) off his chains of slavery (*bondage*) and received with joy (*embrace*) his unchecked (*uncontrolled*) liberty (*enfranchisement*), precious as gold, than my mind (*soul*), now dancing with joy, comes solemnly (*doth celebrate*) to this battle, which I shall enjoy as a feast".
46 *of happy years*, for yourselves.
47 *gentle and as jocund* – "quiet (*gentle*) and as cheerful (*jocund*)".
48 *quiet breast* – "heart which is calm and free from fear".
49 *securely . . . couchéd* – "confident (*securely*) of your victory I see truth (*Virtue*) and courage (*valour*), waiting like an animal ready to spring (*couchéd*) . . .".
50 *trial* – "the fight which is to test their truth".

GAUNT

God in thy good cause make thee prosperous![40]
Be swift like lightning in the execution,[41]
And let thy blows, doubly redoubled,
Fall like amazing thunder on the casque
Of thy adverse pernicious enemy.[42]
Rouse up thy youthful blood, be valiant, and live!

BOLINGBROKE

Mine innocence, and Saint George to thrive![43]

MOWBRAY

However God or fortune cast my lot,[44]
There lives or dies, true to King Richard's throne,
A loyal, just and upright gentleman:
Never did captive, with a freer heart,
Cast off his chains of bondage, and embrace
His golden uncontrolled enfranchisement,
More than my dancing soul doth celebrate
This feast of battle[45] with mine adversary.
Most mighty liege, and my companion peers,
Take from my mouth the wish of happy years.[46]
As gentle and as jocund[47] as to jest,
Go I to fight: truth hath a quiet breast.[48]

KING RICHARD

Farewell, my lord; securely I espy
Virtue with valour couchéd[49] in thine eye:
Order the trial,[50] Marshal, and begin.

MARSHAL

Harry of Hereford, Lancaster, and Derby,
Receive thy lance, and God defend thy right!

51 *On pain to . . . recreant* – "and if he loses he will be thought untruthful (*false*) and guilty (*recreant*) . . .".
52 *approve* – "prove".
53 *Attending but* – "waiting only for".
54 *Sound trumpets . . . combatants* – "Let the trumpets sound and the men who are to fight (*combatants*) come forward".
55 *charge* – "signal to attack".
56 *Stay . . . down* – "Stop; the king has thrown down his truncheon" (i.e. short staff, *warder*, as a sign that the fight is to be stopped).
57 *by* – "aside".
58 *While we return* – "Until we announce to . . .".

BOLINGBROKE

Strong as a tower in hope, I cry "Amen".

MARSHAL

[*To a* Knight] Go bear this lance to Thomas, Duke of Norfolk.

I HERALD

Harry of Hereford, Lancaster, and Derby,
Stands here for God, his sovereign, and himself,
On pain to be found false and recreant,[51]
To prove the Duke of Norfolk, Thomas Mowbray,
A traitor to his God, his kind, and him,
And dares him to set forward to the fight.

2 HERALD

Here standeth Thomas Mowbray, Duke of Norfolk
On pain to be found false and recreant,
Both to defend himself, and to approve[52]
Henry of Hereford, Lancaster, and Derby,
To God, his sovereign, and to him disloyal:
Courageously, and with a free desire,
Attending but[53] the signal to begin.

MARSHAL

Sound trumpets, and set forward combatants![54]

[A charge[55] sounded

Stay! The king hath thrown his warder down.[56]

KING RICHARD

Let them lay by[57] their helmets and their spears,
And both return back to their chairs again.
Withdraw with us, and let the trumpets sound,
While we return[58] these Dukes what we decree.

[A long flourish

59 *list . . . done* – "listen to what I and my council have decided".
60 *For that* – "So that . . .".
61 *dear* – "precious".
62 *for* – "because".
63 *dire aspect . . . swords* – "dreadful (*dire*) sight (*aspect*) of civil war in which English earth would seem to be ploughed up, not by farmers, but by friends and neighbours fighting each other".
64 *eagle-wingéd pride . . . sleep.* Richard speaks of the pride and ambition of the knights as having the wings of an eagle which seeks to fly high (*sky-aspiring*); the hatred and jealousy (*envy*) of these two rivals has set them on (i.e. made them ready) to start a civil war, as if waking up the young child, peace, which lies quietly sleeping in England's cradle.
65 *Which so roused up . . . blood* – "if this sleep was disturbed (*roused up*) with noisy (*boisterous*) and unmusical (*untuned*) drums and with the terrible (*dreadful*) trumpets' sound (*bray*) cruelly re-echoing (*harsh resounding*), and the harsh (*grating*) clashing together (*shock*) of the iron swords of angry (*wrathful*) men, the beautiful child, peace, might be frightened away from England's quiet territories (*confines*), and the English people might have to walk through streams (*wade*) of their own relatives' (*kindred's*) blood".
66 *upon pain of life . . . banishment* – "under penalty of death if you return before, shall not see again (*regreet*) the English kingdom (*dominions*) until ten summers have ripened the harvests (*enriched our fields*), but shall live in exile in foreign countries (*stranger paths*)".
67 *doom* – "sentence".
68 *sly, slow hours . . . exile* – "hours which move with cunning (*sly*) slowness shall never bring to an end (*determinate*) the continuing time (*dateless limit*) of your sorrowful (*dear*) exile".

Draw near,
And list what, with our council, we have done.[59]
For that[60] our kingdom's earth should not be soiled
With that dear[61] blood which it hath fostered,
And for[62] our eyes do hate the dire aspect
Of civil wounds ploughed up with neighbours' swords,[63]
And for we think the eagle-wingéd pride
Of sky-aspiring and ambitious thoughts,
With rival-hating envy, set on you
To wake our peace, which in our country's cradle
Draws the sweet infant breath of gentle sleep;[64]
Which so roused up with boisterous untuned drums,
With harsh resounding trumpets' dreadful bray,
And grating shock of wrathful iron arms,
Might from our quiet confines fright fair peace,
And make us wade even in our kindred's blood:[65]
Therefore, we banish you our territories.
You, Cousin Hereford, upon pain of life,
Till twice five summers have enriched our fields,
Shall not regreet our fair dominions,
But tread the stranger paths of banishment.[66]

BOLINGBROKE

Your will be done. This must my comfort be,
That sun that warms you here shall shine on me,
And those his golden beams, to you here lent,
Shall point on me and gild my banishment.

KING RICHARD

Norfolk, for thee remains a heavier doom,[67]
Which I with some unwillingness pronounce.
The sly, slow hours shall not determinate
The dateless limit of thy dear exile.[68]
The hopeless word of "Never to return"
Breathe I against thee, upon pain of life.

69 *all unlooked for* – "quite unexpected".

70 *A dearer merit . . . air* – "A better reward (*dearer merit*), not so crippling a punishment as to be sent away to any place in the world . . ." (*maim* is usually a verb, "to cripple"; *common*, "belonging to all the world").

71 *my tongue's use . . . harmony* – (I cannot speak in the music of other languages.) "my tongue is no more use to me than a viol or a harp with no strings; it is like a delicate (*cunning*) musical instrument which is fastened (*cased*) up, or, supposing it is open, in the hands of someone who has not learned how to play (*touch*) it to make music (*harmony*)."

72 *engaoled* – "imprisoned".

73 *portcullised with* – "barred, fastened in by"; (*portcullis*, net-work of iron bars hung above the gate of a castle and lowered during attack).

74 *dull, unfeeling . . . on me* – "not knowing the language (*ignorance*) will make me stupid (*dull*), unable to feel what is going on (*unfeeling*), useless (*barren*); this ignorance will be like a prison-guard watching me". (Because I do not know their languages I shall think foreign countries are a prison.)

75 *What is . . . breath* – "Does not your sentence which forbids me to breathe my own country's air (*native breath*) so as to speak the English language condemn me to a silence which is like death?"

76 *It boots . . . compassionate.* – "It is no good asking for pity".

77 *plaining* – "complaining".

78 *take an oath with thee* – "swear an oath before you go".

Doubly portcullised[73] with my teeth and lips

MOWBRAY

A heavy sentence, my most sovereign liege,
And all unlooked for[69] from your highness' mouth!
A dearer merit, not so deep a maim
As to be cast forth in the common air,[70]
Have I deservéd at your highness' hands.
The language I have learned these forty years,
My native English, now I must forgo,
And now my tongue's use is to me no more
Than an unstringéd viol or a harp,
Or like a cunning instrument cased up,
Or, being open, put into his hands
That knows no touch to tune the harmony.[71]
Within my mouth you have engaoled[72] my tongue,
Doubly portcullised[73] with my teeth and lips;
And dull, unfeeling, barren ignorance,
Is made my gaoler to attend on me.[74]
I am too old to fawn upon a nurse,
Too far in years to be a pupil now.
What is thy sentence then but speechless death,
Which robs my tongue from breathing native breath?[75]

KING RICHARD

It boots thee not to be compassionate.[76]
After our sentence, plaining[77] comes too late.

MOWBRAY

Then thus I turn me from my country's light
To dwell in solemn shades of endless night.

[*He moves away*

KING RICHARD

Return again, and take an oath with thee.[78]
Lay on our royal sword your banished hands;
Swear by the duty that you owe to God –

79 *Our part . . . yourselves* – "I do not ask you, now that you have been banished, to swear by the duty you owe to me".

80 *administer* – "say over to you".

81 *embrace . . . love* – "become friends".

82 *regreet nor reconcile . . . hate* – "greet each other again, nor change to friendship (*reconcile*) this storm (*tempest*) which threatens (*louring*) from the hatred you have felt for each other at home in England (*home-bred hate*)".

83 *by advisèd purpose* – "by a plan made purposely (*advisèd*)".

84 *complot any ill* – "plan together any evil".

85 *so fare . . . enemy* – "I cannot say farewell. May things turn out for you (*fare*) as I would wish them to turn out for my enemy".

86 *had* – "would have".

87 *this frail sepulchre of our flesh.* Bolingbroke speaks as if the soul of a living man is buried in the fragile tomb (*frail sepulchre*) of the body (*flesh*).

88 *if ever . . . life* – "if ever I have been disloyal to the king, may my name be rubbed out from the book of those who will have eternal life".

89 *rue* – "be sorry (when he finds out your true character)".

90 *stray . . . way* – "go wrong (*stray*); except (*save*) back to England any way in the world is the right way for me".

Our part therein we banish with yourselves –[79]
To keep the oath that we administer:[80]
You never shall, so help you truth and God,
Embrace each other's love[81] in banishment,
Nor never look upon each other's face;
Nor never write, regreet, nor reconcile
This louring tempest of your home-bred hate,[82]
Nor never by advisèd purpose[83] meet,
To plot, contrive, or complot any ill,[84]
'Gainst us, our state, our subjects, or our land.

BOLINGBROKE

I swear.

MOWBRAY

And I, to keep all this.

BOLINGBROKE

Norfolk, so fare, as to mine enemy:[85]
By this time, had the king permitted us,
One of our souls had[86] wandered in the air,
Banished this frail sepulchre of our flesh,[87]
As now our flesh is banished from this land.
Confess thy treasons, ere thou fly this realm;
Since thou hast far to go, bear not along
The clogging burden of a guilty soul.

MOWBRAY

No, Bolingbroke: if ever I were traitor,
My name be blotted from the book of life,[88]
And I from heaven banished, as from hence;
But what thou art, God, thou, and I do know,
And all too soon, I fear, the king shall rue.[89]
Farewell, my liege, now no way can I stray;
Save back to England, all the world 's my way.[90]

[*Exit*

91 *glasses* – "tears which seem like mirrors".

92 *thy sad aspect . . . spent* – "your sad look (*aspect*) has persuaded me to take away four years from his sentence. After six cheerless (*frozen*) winters have passed (*spent*) . . .".

93 *lies in* – "is contained in".

94 *wanton* – "gay and unashamed".

95 *in regard of me* – "out of consideration (*regard*) for me".

96 *vantage . . . thereby* – "advantage shall I gain or harvest".

97 *bring their times about . . . son* – "bring their seasons (*times*) back again (*about*) for the following year, my lamp of life, which has no oil left in it, and whose light has been used up (*-bewasted*) by time, will have gone out (*be extinct*), as my age gives way to death (*endless night*): the little that is left (*inch*) of my life's candle (*taper*) will have finished burning, and death will cover (*blindfold*) my eyes so that I shall never see my son again". (Gaunt speaks as if death, which will blindfold him, is itself blindfolded – perhaps because death does not want to see and feel pity.)

98 *sullen* – "silent and full of grief".

99 *to furrow me* – "to make lines on my face (as a plough makes furrows on the earth)".

100 *stop no wrinkle . . . breath* – "as time goes on his slow way to bring me to heaven (*in his pilgrimage*), you cannot stop one line (*wrinkle*) from forming on my face. As king you can, if you wish, have me put to death (either by execution or by killing me with grief at my son's banishment); your word is current coinage to buy me death, but, once I am dead, all that you have cannot buy back life (*breath*) for me".

KING RICHARD

Uncle, even in the glasses[91] of thine eyes
I see thy grievéd heart; thy sad aspect
Hath from the number of his banished years
Plucked four away. [*To* BOLINGBROKE] Six frozen winters spent,[92]
Return with welcome, home from banishment.

BOLINGBROKE

How long a time lies in[93] one little word!
Four lagging winters and four wanton[94] springs
End in a word; such is the breath of kings.

GAUNT

I thank my liege, that in regard of me[95]
He shortens four years of my son's exile;
But little vantage shall I reap thereby.[96]
For ere the six years that he hath to spend
Can change their moons and bring their times about,
My oil-dried lamp, and time-bewasted light
Shall be extinct with age and endless night:
My inch of taper will be burnt and done,
And blindfold death not let me see my son.[97]

KING RICHARD

Why, uncle, thou hast many years to live.

GAUNT

But not a minute, king, that thou canst give;
Shorten my days thou canst with sullen[98] sorrow,
And pluck nights from me, but not lend a morrow.
Thou canst help time to furrow me[99] with age,
But stop no wrinkle in his pilgrimage.
Thy word is current with him for my death,
But dead, thy kingdom cannot buy my breath.[100]

101 *upon good advice . . . gave* – "after serious consideration (*advice*), and you gave your vote for, and had a share (*party-*) in this sentence (*verdict*)".

102 *lour* – "look angry and sad".

103 *Things sweet . . . urged me* – "What we think will be quite pleasant may turn out to be (*prove*) unbearable. You pressed me to give my opinion (*urged me*) . . .".

104 *To smooth . . . avoid* – "I would have been kinder (*more mild*) and tried to smooth over what he had done wrong. I was trying (*sought*) not to be called one who favoured his son . . .".

105 *I looked when* – "I expected that".

106 *to make mine own away* – "to destroy my own son".

107 *his train* – "those in attendance on him".

108 *What presence . . . show* – "Let me know from your letters (*paper*) where you are living; I cannot hear it from you in person (*presence*)".

109 *As far as land will let me* – "to the coast".

110 *hoard thy words* – "keep back your words as if they are treasure".

KING RICHARD

Thy son is banished upon good advice,
Whereto thy tongue a party-verdict gave.[101]
Why at our justice seem'st thou then to lour?[102]

GAUNT

Things sweet to taste prove in digestion sour:
You urged me[103] as a judge, but I had rather
You would have bid me argue like a father.
Oh, had it been a stranger, not my child,
To smooth his fault I should have been more mild.
A partial slander sought I to avoid,[104]
And in the sentence my own life destroyed.
Alas, I looked when[105] some of you should say
I was too strict to make mine own away;[106]
But you gave leave to my unwilling tongue,
Against my will, to do myself this wrong.

KING RICHARD

Cousin, farewell; and, uncle, bid him so:
Six years we banish him, and he shall go.
[*Flourish. Exeunt* KING RICHARD *and his train*[107]

AUMERLE

Cousin, farewell. What presence must not know,
From where you do remain, let paper show.[108]

MARSHAL

My lord, no leave take I, for I will ride
As far as land will let me,[109] by your side.

GAUNT

Oh, to what purpose dost thou hoard thy words[110]
That thou return'st no greeting to thy friends?

111 *I have too few . . . heart* – "Although it is the duty (*office*) of the tongue to be wasteful (*prodigal*) of words to speak (*breathe*) the great sorrow (*abundant dolour*) of my heart, I can hardly speak to say good-bye (*take leave*) to you".

112 *Thy grief . . . absence* – "What you have to be sorry for (*grief*) is only (*but*) that you will be away . . .".

113 *when I miscall it . . . pilgrimage* – "when I give it that wrong name, for my heart thinks it a weary journey I am forced to take as penance".

114 *Esteem a foil . . . return* – "try to think of as (*Esteem*) a contrasting setting (*foil*) in which your home-coming is to be placed like a precious stone"; (*foil*, setting of a jewel which shows it to great advantage).

115 *Will but remember . . . jewels* – "will only (*but*) remind (*remember*) me how far I am away from the precious stones (*jewels*) of England . . .".

116 *apprenticehood . . . grief* – "period of training (*apprenticehood*) in foreign travel, and finally, when the training and my sentence are finished (*having my freedom*), I shall only be able to say that I have been a traveller, and a day-worker, in sorrow". (Bolingbroke is using the words *freedom* and *journeyman* in two senses. An apprentice (i.e. a boy or young man learning a trade) was made "free" when his training was finished and he then became a "journeyman" (i.e. a worker paid by the day). Bolingbroke will have his freedom, in a second sense, when his banishment is over; in exile he is a man on a journey.)

BOLINGBROKE

I have too few to take my leave of you,
When the tongue's office should be prodigal,
To breathe the abundant dolour of the heart.[111]

GAUNT

Thy grief is but thy absence[112] for a time.

BOLINGBROKE

Joy absent, grief is present for that time.

GAUNT

What is six winters? They are quickly gone.

BOLINGBROKE

To men in joy, but grief makes one hour ten.

GAUNT

Call it a travel that thou tak'st for pleasure.

BOLINGBROKE

My heart will sigh when I miscall it so,
Which finds it an enforcéd pilgrimage.[113]

GAUNT

The sullen passage of thy weary steps
Esteem a foil, wherein thou art to set
The precious jewel of thy home return.[114]

BOLINGBROKE

Nay, rather, every tedious stride I make,
Will but remember me what deal of world
I wander from the jewels[115] that I love.
Must I not serve a long apprenticehood,
To foreign passages, and in the end,
Having my freedom, boast of nothing else,
But that I was a journeyman to grief?[116]

117 *All places . . . necessity* – "All places under the sun (*that the eye of heaven visits*) are safe and pleasant harbours (*havens*) to a sensible man. Learn to argue like this (*reason thus*) since you have to leave England; nothing gives a man strength (*virtue*) so much as having to do a certain thing (*necessity*)."

118 *Woe doth . . . borne* – "If sorrow can see (*perceives*) that a man is enduring it with only a faint heart (*but faintly borne*), it will press down harder (*heavier sit*) on him".

119 *forth to purchase* – "abroad to win . . .".

120 *Devouring pestilence . . . our air* – "the air in England is thick with deadly plague".

121 *clime* – "climate".

122 *Look what* – "Whatever".

123 *the presence strewed* – "the presence-chamber of the king (where he received his guests and members of his court) with its floor covered (*strewed*) with fresh rushes"; (*rush*, "tall grass-like plant which grows in wet places". The dried leaves were used for laying on floors).

124 *measure or a dance* – "stately dance (*measure*) or a dance of any kind".

125 *gnarling* – "growling (like a dog)".

126 *sets it light* – "cares little for it".

127 *on the frosty Caucasus . . . feast?* – "about the frozen mountains of the Caucasus (mountains in the east of Europe); or satisfy, until a man can eat no more (*cloy*), the biting pain (*hungry edge*) of his wish for food (*appetite*) only by seeing in the mind's eye (*by bare imagination*) the picture of a splendid meal?"

128 *fantastic summer's heat* – "the very great (*fantastic*) heat of an imaginary (*fantastic*) summer".

129 *apprehension . . . sore* – "thinking about (*apprehension of*) pleasure only (*but*) makes a person feel the want of it (*worse*) more keenly. The tooth of cruel (*fell*) grief is never more painful (*doth never rankle more*) than when it bites the sore place but without bursting open the boil (and so lessening the pain by letting out the matter which is inside)". Bolingbroke thinks it is useless to pretend – a man cannot bear burning, or hunger, or cold by pretending he feels the opposite. Sorrow is easier to bear if he lets it be expressed.

GAUNT

All places that the eye of heaven visits,
Are to a wise man ports and happy havens.
Teach thy necessity to reason thus;
There is no virtue like necessity.[117]
Think not the king did banish thee,
But thou the king. Woe doth the heavier sit,
Where it perceives it is but faintly borne.[118]
Go say I sent thee forth to purchase[119] honour,
And not the king exiled thee; or suppose
Devouring pestilence hangs in our air[120]
And thou art flying to a fresher clime.[121]
Look what[122] thy soul holds dear, imagine it
To lie that way thou go'st, not whence thou com'st.
Suppose the singing birds musicians,
The grass whereon thou tread'st the presence strewed,[123]
The flowers fair ladies, and thy steps no more
Than a delightful measure or a dance;[124]
For gnarling[125] sorrow hath less power to bite
The man that mocks at it, and sets it light.[126]

BOLINGBROKE

Oh, who can hold a fire in his hand
By thinking on the frosty Caucasus?
Or cloy the hungry edge of appetite
By bare imagination of a feast?[127]
Or wallow naked in December snow,
By thinking on fantastic summer's heat?[128]
Oh, no, the apprehension of the good
Gives but the greater feeling to the worse!
Fell sorrow's tooth doth never rankle more
Than when he bites, but lanceth not the sore.[129]

130 *I'll bring thee . . . stay* – "I will come with you for some part of your way. If I were young and had your reason (*cause*) for going, I should not delay (*stay*)".

131 *that bears me yet* – "the earth of England on which I am still standing".

(I.iv) Aumerle describes to the king how he said good-bye to Bolingbroke. Richard shows how much he suspects Bolingbroke of trying to become popular with the ordinary people – as if he were the next heir to the throne. Richard has spent too much and given away too much; now he is short of money for the war against the Irish rebels, and must borrow a large amount; those who supply him will be allowed to gather taxes in return. And if more money is needed, rich men shall be made to give or lend more. News is brought that Gaunt is very ill and wishes the king to come to see him. Richard hopes that Gaunt may die so that he can take his possessions.

1 *We did observe.* The scene begins with the end of a sentence. See line 24.

2 *brought you* – "did you go with".

3 *high* – "the noble . . .".

4 *highway* – "main road".

5 *say, what store of* – "tell us, how many . . .".

6 *Faith, none for me; except* – "Indeed, none, for my part; except that . . .".

7 *Awaked the sleeping rheum . . . tear* – "made our eyes water with the cold, so that, by accident, our insincere (*hollow*) leave-taking was given the honour (*grace*) of a tear"; (*rheum*, "moisture coming from eyes, mouth or nose").

GAUNT

Come, come, my son, I 'll bring thee on thy way:
Had I thy youth and cause, I would not stay.[130]

BOLINGBROKE

Then England's ground, farewell: sweet soil, adieu,
My mother, and my nurse, that bears me yet![131]
Where'er I wander, boast of this I can,
Though banished, yet a true-born Englishman.

[*Exeunt*

Scene IV. The court.

Enter the KING, *with* BAGOT *and* GREEN *at one door, and the* DUKE OF AUMERLE *at another.*

KING RICHARD

We did observe.[1] Cousin Aumerle,
How far brought you[2] high[3] Hereford on his way?

AUMERLE

I brought high Hereford, if you call him so,
But to the next highway,[4] and there I left him.

KING RICHARD

And say, what store of[5] parting tears were shed?

AUMERLE

Faith, none for me; except[6] the north-east wind,
Which then blew bitterly against our faces,
Awaked the sleeping rheum, and so by chance
Did grace our hollow parting with a tear.[7]

KING RICHARD

What said our cousin when you parted with him?

8 *for my heart . . . grave* – "because (*for*) I scorned (*disdainéd*) to use untruly (*profane*) the word 'Farewell', that gave me cunning (*craft*) to pretend (*counterfeit*) to be weighed down with (*oppression*) such sorrow that I could not speak, as if there were a weight of earth over the grave in which my words and my sorrow were buried".

9 *a volume* – "a whole book".

10 *come* – "will come". Richard has other plans, not stated.

11 *Observed . . . affects with him* – "noticed (*Observed*) how he tried to make ordinary people love him: how he seemed to make his way deep (*dive*) into their good-will (*hearts*), with politeness (*courtesy*) which was very friendly (*familiar*) and not proud (*humble*); we noticed what respect (*reverence*) he wasted (*did throw away*) on the poorest servants, trying to win the love of (*Wooing*) poor workmen (*craftsmen*) with the cunning (*craft*) of smiles, and by patiently enduring (*underbearing of*) his bad luck (*fortune*), as if to take their love (*affects*) with him into banishment".

12 *bonnet . . . knee* – "cap to a poor girl who sells oysters; two men who drive a cart for their livings (*draymen*) wish that God may give him good luck; they had the pleasure in return (*the tribute*) of seeing him kneel on his easily bended (*supple*) knee".

13 *As were our England . . . hope* – "as if my kingdom belonged to him after me, and as if he were the next heir our subjects could hope for"; (*in reversion*, "after the death of its owner"; *degree*, "rank", so the nearest in *degree* is the next heir).

14 *which stand out . . . advantage* – "who are in revolt (*stand out*) in Ireland, necessary steps (*manage*) must be taken quickly, before time (*leisure*) gives (*yield*) them more opportunity (*means*) for their getting ahead (*advantage*) . . ."; (*expedient* has two meanings: "necessary" and "quick").

AUMERLE

"Farewell":
And for my heart disdainéd that my tongue
Should so profane the word, that taught me craft
To counterfeit oppression of such grief
That words seemed buried in my sorrow's grave.[8]
Marry, would the word "Farewell" have lengthened hours,
And added years to his short banishment,
He should have had a volume[9] of farewells,
But since it would not, he had none of me.

KING RICHARD

He is our cousin, cousin, but 't is doubt,
When time shall call him home from banishment,
Whether our kinsman come[10] to see his friends.
Ourself, and Bushy, Bagot here and Green
Observed his courtship to the common people;
How he did seem to dive into their hearts,
With humble and familiar courtesy,
What reverence he did throw away on slaves,
Wooing poor craftsmen with the craft of smiles,
And patient under-bearing of his fortune,
As 't were to banish their affects with him.[11]
Off goes his bonnet to an oyster-wench;
A brace of draymen bid God speed him well,
And had the tribute of his supple knee,[12]
With "Thanks, my countrymen, my loving friends",
As were our England in reversion his,
And he our subjects' next degree in hope.[13]

GREEN

Well, he is gone, and with him go these thoughts!
Now for the rebels which stand out in Ireland,
Expedient manage must be made, my liege,
Ere further leisure yield them further means
For their advantage[14], and your highness' loss.

15 *for our coffers . . . furnish us* – "because our treasure chests (*coffers*) have become rather empty (*somewhat light*) as a result of our over-splendid court and generous gifts (*liberal largess*), we must sell to others the right to fix and gather the state taxes (*farm our royal realm*), and the money (*revenue*) these financiers give us will supply what we need (*furnish us*) . . .".

16 *come short* – "is not enough".

17 *blank charters: Whereto* – "official orders (*charters*) with only the name and amount missing (*blank*); on which . . .".

18 *subscribe them* – "write in the names of these rich men".

19 *them after . . . presently* – "the sums of money after us to Ireland to supply our needs, for we will set off for Ireland at once (*presently*)".

20 *grievous sick* – "very seriously ill".

21 *post haste* – "by the swiftest messengers".

22 *The lining of his coffers . . . To deck* – "The money inside his treasure chests shall not only make the lining but the coats as well to dress up (*deck*) . . .".

KING RICHARD

We will ourself in person to this war;
And, for our coffers, with too great a court,
And liberal largess, are grown somewhat light,
We are enforced to farm our royal realm,
The revenue whereof shall furnish us[15]
For our affairs in hand: if that come short,[16]
Our substitutes at home shall have blank charters:
Whereto,[17] when they shall know what men are rich,
They shall subscribe them[18] for large sums of gold,
And send them after to supply our wants;
For we will make for Ireland presently.[19]

Enter BUSHY *with news*

Bushy, what news?

BUSHY

Old John of Gaunt is grievous sick,[20] my lord,
Suddenly taken, and hath sent post haste[21]
To entreat your majesty to visit him.

KING RICHARD

Where lies he?

BUSHY

At Ely House.

KING RICHARD

Now put it, God, in the physician's mind
To help him to his grave immediately!
The lining of his coffers shall make coats
To deck[22] our soldiers for these Irish wars.
Come, gentlemen, let 's all go visit him.
Pray God we may make haste, and come too late.
Amen.

[*Exeunt*

(II.i) John of Gaunt, dying, hopes that he may yet give good advice to his nephew, King Richard, but Gaunt's brother, the Duke of York, believes that the king will go his own foolish way. Gaunt thinks that the king cannot go on spending so much and farming out his taxes, bringing shame to England. He tells Richard that he is ready for his grave, and scolds Richard for his extravagance. Richard is angry; if Gaunt were not his father's brother he would pay with his life for scolding the king in this way. Gaunt answers that Richard has already been responsible for the death of Gloucester; he cannot pretend that he would always spare the lives of his uncles, the sons of Edward III. As Gaunt is carried away to die, York tries to make excuses for him but Richard shows little sorrow when told of Gaunt's death, and declares that he will take all Gaunt's possessions and use the money for his Irish wars. York points out that Bolingbroke is the heir of John of Gaunt and asks how Richard holds his crown except as the heir of his father, the Black Prince. Richard pays no attention to this; he is to sail for Ireland on the next day and York is to be governor of England in his absence. From the words of Northumberland and two other noblemen we learn of the king's unpopularity. We learn too that Bolingbroke is returning from France with three thousand men; after the king has sailed for Ireland he will land in the north of England.

1 *In wholesome counsel . . . youth* – "in good advice (*counsel*) to his wild youth".

2 *strive not with your breath* – "fight to speak (wasting your strength)".

3 *Enforce attention . . . pain* – "compel (*Enforce*) people to listen as if to serious music (*deep harmony*). When men can speak few (*scarce*) words, such words are not often used up (*spent*) without result (*in vain*), for those who speak (*breathe*) when they are in pain speak what is true".

4 *whom youth and ease . . . glose* – "who have grown used to telling pleasing lies (*to glose*) in youth and comfort (*ease*)".

5 *More are men's . . . marked* – "How men die is more noticed (*marked*) . . .".

6 *is sweetest last . . . more* – "is most appreciated at the very end and held in the memory (*Writ in remembrance*) more firmly . . .".

7 *My death's sad tale . . . ear* – "what I say (*tale*) at the sad hour of my death may make him listen".

8 *it is stopped* – "Richard's ear is blocked up . . .".

9 *As praises . . . open ear* – "such as admiration of his splendour: in addition (*then*) there are immoral and exciting (*Lascivious*) poems (*metres*), to whose poisonous (*venom*) sound the ready (*open*) ear . . .".

ACT TWO

Scene I. Ely House.

Enter JOHN OF GAUNT *sick, with the* DUKE OF YORK, *and* Others.

GAUNT

Will the king come, that I may breathe my last,
In wholesome counsel to his unstaid youth?[1]

YORK

Vex not yourself, nor strive not with your breath,[2]
For all in vain comes counsel to his ear.

GAUNT

Oh, but they say the tongues of dying men
Enforce attention like deep harmony.
Where words are scarce, they are seldom spent in vain,
For they breathe truth that breathe their words in pain.[3]
He that no more must say is listened more
Than they whom youth and ease have taught to glose.[4]
More are men's ends marked[5] than their lives before.
The setting sun, and music at the close,
As the last taste of sweets, is sweetest last,
Writ in remembrance more[6] than things long past;
Though Richard my life's counsel would not hear,
My death's sad tale may yet undeaf his ear.[7]

YORK

No, it is stopped[8] with other flattering sounds,
As praises of his state: then there are found
Lascivious metres, to whose venom sound
The open ear[9] of youth doth always listen;

10 *our tardy apish nation . . . imitation* – "our English people, copying like unintelligent monkeys (*apish*) when the fashion is over (*tardy*), come lamely following in unworthy (*base*) imitation"; (*tardy*, "late"; *Limps*, "walks lamely").

11 *thrust forth a vanity . . . vile* – "put out on show a piece of idle folly – so long as it is new there is no thought (*respect*) of how evil it is –".

12 *Where will . . . wit's regard* – "where a man's wish for pleasure (*will*) fights against the authority of (*doth mutiny with*) all considerations (*regard*) of common sense (*wit*)".

13 *rash fierce blaze of riot* – "his spending money so fast (*riot*) like a dangerous quickly blazing fire . . .".

14 *Small showers* – "showers of soft rain".

15 *He tires betimes* – "A rider gets tired soon (*betimes*) . . .".

16 *With eager feeding . . . feeder* – "a man who eats too quickly (*eager*) can choke himself with food". (Richard may "choke" himself with spending too much.)

17 *Light vanity . . . itself* – "Empty (*Light*) foolishness (*vanity*), like a greedy bird who eats all it can get (*cormorant*) and is never satisfied (*insatiate*), eating up (*consuming*) all the ways of raising money (*means*), ends by eating itself".

18 *This royal throne . . . demi-paradise* – "England has been a throne to many great kings; the island is like a king's ceremonial rod of office ('*sceptre*'); it is a land where majesty grows, where Mars, the god of War, has his palace (*seat*); it is a second (*other*) Eden, a half-paradise". (*Eden* or *paradise*, land of happiness in which Adam and Eve first lived.)

19 *Against infection* – "where she could protect herself against plague (*infection*)".

20 *Which serves it . . . house* – "which acts like a protecting wall or like a deep channel of water (*moat*) dug round a house to defend it . . .".

21 *This nurse . . . breed* – "where great kings have been born and brought up, feared on account of (*by*) their race (*breed*)"; (*teeming*, "ready to give birth").

Or as a moat defensive to a house[20]

Report of fashions in proud Italy,
Whose manners still our tardy apish nation
Limps after in base imitation.[10]
Where doth the world thrust forth a vanity –
So it be new, there 's no respect how vile –[11]
That is not quickly buzzed into his ears?
Then all too late comes counsel to be heard,
Where will doth mutiny with wit's regard.[12]
Direct not him whose way himself will choose,
'T is breath thou lack'st, and that breath wilt thou lose.

GAUNT

Methinks I am a prophet new inspired,
And thus expiring do foretell of him
His rash fierce blaze of riot[13] cannot last,
For violent fires soon burn out themselves;
Small showers[14] last long, but sudden storms are short.
He tires betimes[15] that spurs too fast betimes;
With eager feeding, food doth choke the feeder.[16]
Light vanity, insatiate cormorant,
Consuming means, soon preys upon itself.[17]
This royal throne of kings, this sceptered isle,
This earth of majesty, this seat of Mars,
This other Eden, demi-paradise;[18]
This fortress built by Nature for herself,
Against infection[19] and the hand of war;
This happy breed of men, this little world,
This precious stone, set in the silver sea,
Which serves it in the office of a wall,
Or as a moat defensive to a house,[20]
Against the envy of less happier lands;
This blesséd plot, this earth, this realm, this England,
This nurse, this teeming womb of royal kings,
Feared by their breed,[21] and famous by their birth,
Renownéd for their deeds as far from home,

22 *Renownéd . . . ransom* – "having won fame (*Renownéd*) for deeds of true knighthood (*chivalry*) in the service of Christ (*Christian*) even as far away as Jerusalem where, in the land of Jews (*Jewry*) who are too fixed in opinion (*stubborn*) to become followers of Christ, there is the stone tomb (*sepulchre*) of the one who paid his price to set the world free (*ransom*)".

23 *dear* – "precious".

24 *pelting* – "of little value". The king has "leased out" his power by selling to others the right to tax the people.

25 *England . . . bonds.* The sea which encircles England could feel triumph at protecting England's coasts; the rocks of the sea shore fight back against the jealous (*envious*) king of the sea (*watery Neptune*) which seems to besiege us; but now England is free no longer; she is held down by shameful legal agreements (*bound in with shame*), with shameful stains (*blots*) of ink; her bonds (or prisoner's chains) are bonds (of parchment), on which the king has written his shameful (*rotten*) bargains.

26 *was wont to* – "used to".

27 *would the scandal . . . death.* Gaunt would die happily if his death would end England's disgrace.

28 *hot colts . . . the more* – "hot-tempered ungrown horses, when they are checked (*raged*), become more wild".

29 *fares* – "is, is getting on . . .".

30 *What comfort* – "How are you . . .".

31 *befits my composition* – "suits what I am".

32 *gaunt* – "thin and ill".

33 *Within me.* Gaunt gives three reasons for his thinness: not eating the food of joy; not sleeping, so as to watch over England; missing the food which fathers have – the sight of their children.

34 *kept a tedious fast* – "not eaten for a long and tiring (*tedious*) time".

watery Neptune

For Christian service, and true chivalry,
As is the sepulchre in stubborn Jewry
Of the world's ransom,[22] blesséd Mary's son.
This land of such dear[23] souls, this dear, dear land,
Dear for her reputation through the world,
Is now leased out – I die pronouncing it –
Like to a tenement or pelting[24] farm.
England, bound in with the triumphant sea,
Whose rocky shore beats back the envious siege
Of watery Neptune, is now bound in with shame,
With inky blots, and rotten parchment bonds.[25]
That England, that was wont to[26] conquer others,
Hath made a shameful conquest of itself.
Ah, would the scandal vanish with my life,
How happy then were my ensuing death![27]

Enter KING RICHARD *and* QUEEN, AUMERLE, BUSHY, GREEN, BAGOT, ROSS, *and* WILLOUGHBY.

YORK

The king is come; deal mildly with his youth,
For young hot colts, being raged, do rage the more![28]

QUEEN

How fares[29] our noble Uncle Lancaster?

KING RICHARD

What comfort,[30] man? How is 't with agéd Gaunt?

GAUNT

Oh, how that name befits my composition![31]
Old Gaunt, indeed, and gaunt[32] in being old.
Within me[33] grief hath kept a tedious fast,[34]

35 *For sleeping England . . . watched* – "to protect England, and also to watch for the hour when England will wake again and become great, I have for a long time stayed awake".

36 *Is my strict fast* – "I am kept from, by something that has to be obeyed exactly (*strict*) (i.e. the king's sentence of banishment on Bolingbroke)".

37 *Gaunt* – "Ready".

38 *gaunt . . . bones* – "thin and deathlike as a grave itself which contains (*inherits*) only (*nought but*) bones in an empty (*hollow*) birth-cave (*womb*) of death".

39 *Can sick men . . . names* – "Are you really so ill when you use so exactly (*nicely*) in making puns all the meanings of this word 'gaunt' which is your name?"

40 *No, misery . . . in me* – "No, I am not pretending to be ill but my suffering (*misery*) finds amusement (*makes sport*) in laughing at itself (*to mock itself*). Because you want my family name to die out (and have banished my heir) . . . ".

41 *men living . . . that die* – "it is usual for those who are healthy to flatter the dying by pretending that they will get better".

42 *a-dying* – "in the act of dying".

And who abstains from meat that is not gaunt?
For sleeping England long time have I watched;[35]
Watching breeds leanness, leanness is all gaunt.
The pleasure that some fathers feed upon
Is my strict fast[36] – I mean, my children's looks –
And therein fasting, hast thou made me gaunt.
Gaunt[37] am I for the grave, gaunt as a grave,
Whose hollow womb inherits nought but bones.[38]

KING RICHARD

Can sick men play so nicely with their names?[39]

GAUNT

No, misery makes sport to mock itself.
Since thou dost seek to kill my name in me,[40]
I mock my name, great king, to flatter thee.

KING RICHARD

Should dying men flatter with those that live?

GAUNT

No, no; men living flatter those that die.[41]

KING RICHARD

Thou, now a-dying,[42] say'st thou flatterest me.

GAUNT

Oh no, thou diest, though I the sicker be!

KING RICHARD

I am in health; I breathe, and see thee ill.

43 *Ill in myself . . . reputation sick* – "I, who see you, am myself ill and, as I look at you, I see a man who is ill. But the bed on which you lie dying is the whole of England and your illness is in what your people think of you (*reputation*)".

44 *Commit'st thy anointed body . . . thee* – "trust those doctors (*physicians*) to cure you who first made you ill". A patient's body might be rubbed with oil (*anointed*) as a cure; a king's head is sprinkled with holy oil (*anointed*) when he is crowned. So Richard is trying to cure his money difficulties by trusting his power to his favourites who first caused his troubles.

45 *A thousand flatterers . . . land* – "Although the area (*compass*) which a crown contains is very small, the power of a king is great, and, to the many flatterers who surround him (*sit within thy crown*), Richard has given his power, so that the overspending (*waste*) of the state's money extends over the whole country (*is no whit lesser than thy land*), although the crown itself contains only a small space (*encagéd in so small a verge*)"; (*no whit*, "not *at all*". Gaunt may also be playing with the sense of "no wit" inside the king's *crown*, i.e. "head").

46 *grandsire* – "grandfather", i.e. Edward III.

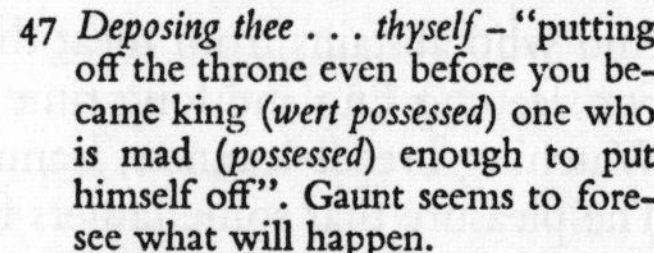

47 *Deposing thee . . . thyself* – "putting off the throne even before you became king (*wert possessed*) one who is mad (*possessed*) enough to put himself off". Gaunt seems to foresee what will happen.

48 *wert thou regent . . . land* – "supposing that you were the ruler (*regent*) of the whole world, it would be (*were*) a disgraceful thing to rent out (*let . . . by lease*) England; but when England is all you have for your kingdom (*thy world*) . . .".

49 *Thy state of law . . . law* – "Your duty to govern (*state of law*) has been handed over to others by legal agreement".

50 *A lunatic, lean-witted . . . admonition* – "A mad fool, whose intelligence (and not only his body) is thin, trusting to (*Presuming on*) the freedom (*privilege*) to speak which a fit of fever (*ague*) seems to give you, do you dare with the cold rebuke (*frozen admonition*) of a man who is almost cold in death . . .".

51 *seat's* – "throne's".

52 *great Edward's son*, the Black Prince (Richard's father) son of Edward III.

53 *This tongue . . . shoulders* – "Because of your tongue which scolds so outspokenly, I would cut off your disrespectful (*unreverent*) head"; (*roundly*, "outspokenly, in a scolding way").

great Edward's son[52]

GAUNT

Now he that made me knows I see thee ill:
Ill, in myself, to see, and in thee, seeing ill.
Thy death-bed is no lesser than thy land,
Wherein thou liest, in reputation sick,[43]
And thou, too careless patient as thou art,
Commit'st thy anointed body to the cure
Of those physicians that first wounded thee.[44]
A thousand flatterers sit within thy crown,
Whose compass is no bigger than thy head,
And yet, encagéd in so small a verge,
The waste is no whit lesser than thy land.[45]
Oh, had thy grandsire[46] with a prophet's eye,
Seen how his son's son should destroy his sons,
From forth thy reach he would have laid thy shame,
Deposing thee before thou wert possessed,
Which art possessed now to depose thyself.[47]
Why, cousin, wert thou regent of the world,
It were a shame to let this land by lease;
But, for thy world enjoying but this land,[48]
Is it not more than shame to shame it so?
Landlord of England art thou now, not king:
Thy state of law is bondslave to the law,[49]
And thou –

KING RICHARD

A lunatic, lean-witted fool,
Presuming on an ague's privilege,
Dar'st with thy frozen admonition[50]
Make pale our cheek, chasing the royal blood
With fury, from his native residence!
Now, by my seat's[51] right royal majesty,
Wert thou not brother to great Edward's son,[52]
This tongue that runs so roundly in thy head
Should run thy head from thy unreverent shoulders.[53]

54 *my brother . . . son* – "because your father (Edward, the Black Prince) was my brother, and our father was Edward III".

55 *pelican.* A bird believed to peck its own chest and let out its blood for its young birds to feed on.

56 *That blood already . . . Hast thou . . . caroused* – "the blood of an uncle you have already drawn off or let flow (*tapped out*) and, like a drunkard, you have gladly drunk it down (*caroused*)".

57 *Whom fair befall . . . souls* – "may he have joy in heaven among the souls of the blessed".

58 *May be a precedent* – "may serve as an example to show the rule (*precedent*) which you follow . . .".

59 *thou respect'est not* – "are not held back by any consideration from".

60 *thy unkindness . . . crop* – "let your cruelty be like bent (*crookéd*) old age, or like time with his sickle, to cut down (*crop*) . . .". (*crookéd age* may have two meanings: "age which makes a man bowed down" and "Time who carries a sickle" – i.e. a curved knife used for cutting grass etc.)

61 *Love they to live* – "Let those desire to go on living . . .".

62 *sullens* – "moods of ill-temper".

63 *become* – "are suitable for".

64 *wayward sickliness* – "illness (*sickliness*) which makes him easily angered like a wilful (*wayward*) child".

65 *holds you dear . . . is.* York means that Gaunt loves Richard as much as he would love his son Bolingbroke, if Bolingbroke were present. Richard agrees, but chooses to misunderstand – Gaunt loves him, he says, as much as Bolingbroke does, i.e. not at all; just as they have no love for him, he has none for them: let things go on as they are.

That blood already, like the pelican,[55]
Hast thou tapped out, and drunkenly caroused[56]

GAUNT

Oh, spare me not, my brother Edward's son,
For that I was his father Edward's son;[54]
That blood already, like the pelican,[55]
Hast thou tapped out, and drunkenly caroused.[56]
My brother Gloucester, plain well-meaning soul –
Whom fair befall in heaven 'mongst happy souls –[57]
May be a precedent[58] and witness good,
That thou respect'st not[59] spilling Edward's blood.
Join with the present sickness that I have,
And thy unkindness be like crookéd age,
To crop[60] at once a too-long withered flower.
Live in thy shame, but die not shame with thee!
These words hereafter thy tormentors be!
Convey me to my bed, then to my grave.
Love they to live[61] that love and honour have.

[*Exit, borne off by his* Attendants

KING RICHARD

And let them die that age and sullens[62] have;
For both hast thou, and both become[63] the grave.

YORK

I do beseech your majesty, impute his words
To wayward sickliness[64] and age in him:
He loves you, on my life, and holds you dear
As Harry, Duke of Hereford, were he here.

KING RICHARD

Right, you say true: as Hereford's love, so his;
As theirs, so mine: and all be as it is.[65]

Enter NORTHUMBERLAND

NORTHUMBERLAND

My liege, old Gaunt commends him to your majesty.

66 *a stringless instrument* – "like a harp, etc. which is silent because the strings are broken".

67 *bankrupt.* A bankrupt is one who has spent too much (and cannot pay his debts). York hopes that he may be the next, like Gaunt, to have *spent* life and all.

68 *The ripest fruit first falls* – "We must expect the old (*ripest fruit*) to die (*falls*) before younger men".

69 *our pilgrimage must be* – "we also are going on a long journey to the holy place of death (*pilgrimage*), and that journey must one day be ended".

70 *supplant those rough . . . privilege* – "drive out (*supplant*) those wild (*rough*), rough-haired (*rug-headed*) Irish foot-soldiers (*kerns*), who live like poison where no other poisonous thing is allowed . . .". (St. Patrick of Ireland was said to have driven out all snakes from that country.)

71 *ask some charge* – "require some expense".

72 *seize to us . . . moveables* – "take for myself the silver and gold dishes (*plate*), money, income and all kinds of furniture (*moveables*) . . .".

73 *tender duty* – "the duty to a king which a tender conscience feels".

74 *Nor Gaunt's rebukes . . . wrongs* – "Neither the king's rebuking of Gaunt, nor acts of injustice to individual Englishmen".

75 *the prevention of . . . marriage.* When Bolingbroke, after the death of his first wife, was engaged to a cousin of the French king (Richard's father-in-law), Richard persuaded the king not to allow the marriage.

76 *sour my patient cheek . . . wrinkle* – "look with anger instead of patience, or frown at all . . .".

those rough rug-headed kerns

KING RICHARD

What says he?

NORTHUMBERLAND

Nay, nothing, all is said.
His tongue is now a stringless instrument;[66]
Words, life, and all, old Lancaster hath spent.

YORK

Be York the next that must be bankrupt[67] so!
Though death be poor, it ends a mortal woe.

KING RICHARD

The ripest fruit first falls,[68] and so doth he;
His time is spent, our pilgrimage must be.[69]
So much for that! Now for our Irish wars:
We must supplant those rough rug-headed kerns,
Which live like venom, where no venom else
But only they have privilege[70] to live.
And, for these great affairs do ask some charge,[71]
Towards our assistance we do seize to us
The plate, coin, revenues, and moveables,[72]
Whereof our Uncle Gaunt did stand possessed.

YORK

How long shall I be patient? Oh, how long
Shall tender duty[73] make me suffer wrong?
Not Gloucester's death, nor Hereford's banishment,
Nor Gaunt's rebukes, nor England's private wrongs,[74]
Nor the prevention of poor Bolingbroke
About his marriage,[75] nor my own disgrace,
Have ever made me sour my patient cheek,
Or bend one wrinkle[76] on my sovereign's face.

77 *Accomplished . . . hours* – "when he was of your age"; (*Accomplished with*, "having reached").

78 *far gone with* – "carried too far by".

79 *compare between* – "make this comparison between the king and his father".

80 *What 's the matter?* Richard has not been listening.

81 *I, pleased . . . all* – "I must speak without permission and be content to take my punishment".

82 *gripe* – "take fiercely".

83 *royalties* – "grants made by the king to a noble and to his heirs".

84 *Take Hereford's . . . rights* – "If you take away from Bolingbroke his right to inherit from his father, then you take away the right of every thing in time to follow another in the usual (*customary*) way". York speaks as if time also has *charters*.

85 *But by fair sequence* – "except by being allowed to inherit your father's place in an honourable (*fair*) way".

86 *afore God*, "before God; as God knows".

I am the last of noble Edward's sons,
Of whom thy father, Prince of Wales, was first.
In war was never lion raged more fierce:
In peace was never gentle lamb more mild
Than was that young and princely gentleman.
His face thou hast, for even so looked he,
Accomplished with the number of thy hours;[77]
But when he frowned, it was against the French,
And not against his friends; his noble hand
Did win what he did spend, and spent not that
Which his triumphant father's hand had won:
His hands were guilty of no kindred blood,
But bloody with the enemies of his kin:
Oh, Richard, York is too far gone with[78] grief,
Or else he never would compare between![79]

KING RICHARD

Why, Uncle, what 's the matter?[80]

YORK

Oh, my liege,
Pardon me, if you please; if not, I, pleased
Not to be pardoned, am content with all:[81]
Seek you to seize and gripe[82] into your hands
The royalties[83] and rights of banished Hereford?
Is not Gaunt dead and doth not Hereford live?
Was not Gaunt just and is not Harry true?
Did not the one deserve to have an heir?
Is not his heir a well-deserving son?
Take Hereford's rights away, and take from time
His charters, and his customary rights:[84]
Let not tomorrow then ensue today:
Be not thyself. For how art thou a king
But by fair sequence[85] and succession?
Now, afore[86] God – God forbid I say true –
If you do wrongfully seize Hereford's rights,

87 *Call in . . . offered homage* – "take back (*Call in*) the rights you have given him in written documents (*letters patents*) to ask (*sue*), through officers appointed to look after all his affairs (*attorneys general*), for his inheritance (*livery*), and refuse (*deny*) his promise of loyalty (*offered homage*) by which he has the right to his lands".

88 *a thousand well-disposéd hearts* – "the support of a thousand others who are your friends (*well-disposéd*)".

89 *prick my tender patience* – "drive me too far". York speaks as if his patience is a horse which has been spurred too hard.

90 *by the while* – "here (*by*) while you do it".

91 *by bad courses . . . good* – "of evil actions (*by bad courses*) it is known that their results (*events*) can never turn (*fall*) out well".

92 *repair* – "come".

93 *see* – "see to, look after".

94 *trow* – "believe".

95 *just* – "honourable".

Call in the letters patents that he hath
By his attorneys general to sue
His livery, and deny his offered homage,[87]
You pluck a thousand dangers on your head,
You lose a thousand well-disposéd hearts,[88]
And prick my tender patience[89] to those thoughts
Which honour and allegiance cannot think.

KING RICHARD

Think what you will: we seize into our hands
His plate, his goods, his money and his lands.

YORK

I'll not be by the while![90] My liege, farewell!
What will ensue hereof, there 's none can tell.
But by bad courses may be understood,
That their events can never fall out good.[91]

[*Exit*

KING RICHARD

Go, Bushy, to the Earl of Wiltshire straight;
Bid him repair[92] to us to Ely House,
To see[93] this business. Tomorrow next
We will for Ireland, and 't is time, I trow:[94]
And we create, in absence of ourself,
Our Uncle York, lord governor of England,
For he is just,[95] and always loved us well.
Come on, our queen; tomorrow must we part;
Be merry, for our time of stay is short.

Flourish. Exeunt all except NORTHUMBERLAND, WILLOUGHBY *and* ROSS

NORTHUMBERLAND

Well, lords, the Duke of Lancaster is dead.

96 *Barely in title . . . revenue* – "He has none of the income of the estates (*revenue*) and scarcely has the title".

97 *great* – "ready to burst" (literally "ready to give birth").

98 *Ere 't be disburdened . . . tongue* – "before I free it of its load (– *burden* –) by speaking openly (*with a liberal tongue*)".

99 *Tends . . . speak* – "Does what you would like to say refer . . .".

100 *Bereft . . . patrimony* – "Having lost and had cut off (*gelded*) his inheritance (*patrimony*)".

101 *are borne In him* – "are endured in his case".

102 *moe* – "more".

103 *declining* – "falling from greatness".

104 *inform Merely in hate* – "report as informers only from hatred (without any truth)".

105 *severely prosecute* – "follow up with strict punishment".

ROSS

And living too, for now his son is duke.

WILLOUGHBY

Barely in title, not in revenue.[96]

NORTHUMBERLAND

Richly in both, if justice had her right.

ROSS

My heart is great;[97] but it must break with silence,
Ere 't be disburdened with a liberal tongue.[98]

NORTHUMBERLAND

Nay, speak thy mind; and let him ne'er speak more
That speaks thy words again to do thee harm!

WILLOUGHBY

Tends that thou wouldst speak[99] to the Duke of Hereford?
If it be so, out with it boldly, man!
Quick is mine ear to hear of good towards him.

ROSS

No good at all that I can do for him,
Unless you call it good to pity him,
Bereft and gelded of his patrimony.[100]

NORTHUMBERLAND

Now, afore God, 't is shame such wrongs are borne
In him,[101] a royal prince, and many moe[102]
Of noble blood in this declining[103] land.
The king is not himself, but basely led
By flatterers, and what they will inform
Merely in hate[104] gainst any of us all,
That will the king severely prosecute[105]
'Gainst us, our lives, our children, and our heirs.

106 *The commons . . . taxes* – "He has robbed the common people with heavy (*grievous*) taxation" (*pill*, "to take the skin off").

107 *ancient quarrels* – "past offences against him".

108 *daily . . . what* – "every day new ways of getting money by force (*exactions*) are invented (*devised*), such as blank charters, compulsory gifts (*benevolences*) and I do not know (*wot not*) what else". (The "blank charters" are those spoken of earlier, I.iv.48.)

109 *this* – "this money".

110 *upon compromise* – "by agreement". Richard had given up some of the French towns and territory which had been won by England.

111 *in farm*. In return for paying a fixed sum to the king he has the right to collect taxes.

112 *a broken man* – "a man who has more debts than he has possessions".

113 *dissolution* – "ruin".

114 *But* – "except".

115 *sit sore . . . perish* – "blow hard against our sails, and yet we do not lower them, but, foolishly confident (*securely*), lose the ships and our lives (*perish*)". Northumberland speaks of the danger arising from the king's actions as a great storm at sea.

ROSS

The commons hath he pilled with grievous taxes[106]
And quite lost their hearts: the nobles hath he fined
For ancient quarrels,[107] and quite lost their hearts.

WILLOUGHBY

And daily new exactions are devised,
As blanks, benevolences, and I wot not what.[108]
But what, o' God's name, doth become of this?[109]

NORTHUMBERLAND

Wars hath not wasted it, for warred he hath not,
But basely yielded upon compromise,[110]
That which his ancestors achieved with blows:
More hath he spent in peace than they in wars.

ROSS

The Earl of Wiltshire hath the realm in farm.[111]

WILLOUGHBY

The king 's grown bankrupt like a broken man.[112]

NORTHUMBERLAND

Reproach and dissolution[113] hangeth o'er him.

ROSS

He hath not money for these Irish wars,
His burdenous taxations notwithstanding,
But[114] by the robbing of the banished duke.

NORTHUMBERLAND

His noble kinsman! Most degenerate king!
But, lords, we hear this fearful tempest sing,
Yet seek no shelter to avoid the storm.
We see the wind sit sore upon our sails,
And yet we strike not, but securely perish.[115]

116 *unavoided . . . our wreck* – "by this time (*now*) the danger is unavoidable (*unavoided*) because (*for*) we have tolerated (*suffering*) in this way (*so*) the dangerous actions of the king".

117 *Even through . . . peering* – "There is a sign of hope even when all hope seems lost; I can see (*spy*) the eyes of something living (*life*) looking out secretly (*peering*) through the empty (*hollow*) eye-sockets of a dead man's skull".

118 *but thyself . . . as thoughts* – "no more than (*but*) a part of yourself, and when you speak to us, it seems that you are only silently thinking". (We shall not tell the king; it will be as if you had not spoken.)

119 *thus* – "I will say this".

120 *Brittany* – part of the north-west of France.

121 *intelligence* – "news".

122 *late broke from* – "lately escaped from the house of".

123 *late;* until 1397 when he was banished.

124 *furnished* – "supplied".

125 *tall* – "large".

126 *men of war* – "soldiers".

127 *making hither . . . expedience* – "making their way here with all haste"

128 *mean to touch . . . of the king* – "intend to land in the north; perhaps they would have done so (*had*) before this, except (*but*) that they are waiting until the king has set off first . . .".

129 *our slavish yoke* – "the yoke of slavery which has been on our necks".

tall[125] *ships*

ROSS

We see the very wreck that we must suffer,
And unavoided is the danger now
For suffering so the causes of our wreck.[116]

NORTHUMBERLAND

Not so. Even through the hollow eyes of death,
I spy life peering;[117] but I dare not say
How near the tidings of our comfort is.

WILLOUGHBY

Nay, let us share thy thoughts, as thou dost ours.

ROSS

Be confident to speak, Northumberland!
We three are but thyself, and speaking so,
Thy words are but as thoughts;[118] therefore, be bold.

NORTHUMBERLAND

Then thus:[119] I have from Port le Blanc, a bay
In Brittany,[120] received intelligence,[121]
That Harry, Duke of Hereford, Rainold, Lord Cobham,
That late broke from[122] the Duke of Exeter,
His brother, Archbishop late[123] of Canterbury,
Sir Thomas Erpingham, Sir John Ramston,
Sir John Norbery, Sir Robert Waterton, and Francis Quoint,
All these well furnished[124] by the Duke of Bretagne
With eight tall[125] ships, three thousand men of war[126]
Are making hither with all expedience,[127]
And shortly mean to touch our northern shore;
Perhaps they had ere this, but that they stay
The first departing of the king[128] for Ireland.
If then we shall shake off our slavish yoke,[129]

130 *Imp out* – "fix new feathers on to". So the wing of a falcon (a valuable hunting bird) might be mended.

131 *Redeem . . . crown.* "To pawn" is to get money by leaving with a pawn-broker an article of value, which is given back or "redeemed" when the money is repaid. Northumberland speaks as if Richard, by selling the right to collect taxes, has pawned and damaged (*blemished*) his crown.

132 *our sceptre's gilt* – "the gold of England's sceptre".

133 *in post* – "in haste".

134 *Ravenspurgh.* Once a great port on the Humber.

135 *faint* – "draw back faint-hearted".

136 *urge doubts to them* – "persuade (*urge*) those to hesitate (*doubts*) . . .".

137 *Hold out . . . and* – "If only my horse stays strong . . .".

(II.ii) The Queen is full of sorrow and fear for which she can find no reason. Green brings the news that Bolingbroke has landed and many noblemen have gone to join him. York's son, Aumerle, has set off to rejoin the king and York has no one to help him. His sister-in-law, the Duchess of Gloucester, from whom he hoped to borrow £1000, has just died. York himself is in a difficult position: he is bound to support the authority of the king yet he knows that the king has treated Bolingbroke unjustly. He asks the king's favourites, Bushy, Bagot and Green, to gather what forces they can and meet him at Berkeley Castle in the west of England. Green and Bushy decide to go to Bristol, Bagot will go to Ireland; all three have reason to fear that, as friends of the king, they will be punished for the ways in which they have forced both the common people and the nobles to supply the king with money.

1 *life-harming heaviness . . . disposition* – "sadness (*heaviness*) which is harmful to the body, and welcome, or gladly take on, a cheerful mood (*disposition*)".

2 *ripe* – "ready for birth".

Imp out[130] our drooping country's broken wing,
Redeem from broking pawn the blemished crown,[131]
Wipe off the dust that hides our sceptre's gilt,[132]
And make high majesty look like itself,
Away with me in post[133] to Ravenspurgh;[134]
But if you faint,[135] as fearing to do so,
Stay and be secret, and myself will go.

ROSS

To horse, to horse; urge doubts to them[136] that fear!

WILLOUGHBY

Hold out my horse, and[137] I will first be there!

[*Exeunt*

Scene II. The palace.

Enter QUEEN, BUSHY *and* BAGOT.

BUSHY

Madam, your majesty is too much sad.
You promised, when you parted with the king,
To lay aside life-harming heaviness,
And entertain a cheerful disposition.[1]

QUEEN

To please the king, I did: to please myself
I cannot do it; yet I know no cause
Why I should welcome such a guest as grief,
Save bidding farewell to so sweet a guest
As my sweet Richard; yet again methinks,
Some unborn sorrow, ripe[2] in fortune's womb,
Is coming towards me, and my inward soul
With nothing trembles; at some thing it grieves,
More than with parting from my lord the king.

3 *Each substance . . . Distinguish form* – "With every real reason (*substance*) for sorrow (*of a grief*) there are found twenty reasons which are not real (*shadows*) but which seem so (*shows like grief itself*). For the eyes of a person full of sorrow, as if looking through a glass (*glazed*) of tears which stop her seeing things truly (*blinding*), break up (*divides*) the one real thing in front of her (*one thing entire*) so that it seems like a number of things (*many objects*); in the same way, special glasses for looking through (or, possibly, certain specially made puzzle-pictures, *perspectives*) show only (*but*) a muddle (*confusion*) if one looks straight forward (*rightly gazed upon*), but if one looks sideways (*eyed awry*) from the correct angle, one can see what is really there (*distinguish form*)".

4 *Looking awry . . . not* – "looking from the *wrong* angle (*awry*) at your husband's leaving for Ireland, finds reasons for sorrow (*shapes of grief*), more than just his absence, to cry for (*wail*), but if you look at the thing straight (*as it is*), the other reasons are not true or real (*shadows of what is not*)".

5 *for things true* – "instead of crying for things which are true".

6 *so heavy sad . . . nothing* – "so heavy with sadness as if thinking about this unclear idea (*on no thought*) in my mind (*I think*) makes me for a non-existent sorrow (*with heavy nothing*) . . .".

7 *conceit* – "an idea in the mind, something imaginary".

8 *'T is nothing less . . . possess* – "My sadness is not from any idea in the mind (It has no reason at all). An imaginary sorrow always (*still*) comes (*is derived*) from some earlier (*forefather*) grief; mine is not like that, for nothing has caused or produced (*begot*) my sorrow and yet my sorrow is there (*something*); or perhaps some cause (that I do not yet know about) *has* produced the vague sorrow that I feel (*nothing that I grieve*); the grief I feel now (*do possess*) is actually coming to me later (*in reversion mine*)".

9 *wot* – "know".

Like perspectives, which rightly gazed upon
Show nothing but confusion, eyed awry,
Distinguished form[3]

BUSHY

Each substance of a grief hath twenty shadows
Which shows like grief itself, but is not so.
For sorrow's eye, glazéd with blinding tears,
Divides one thing entire, to many objects;
Like perspectives, which rightly gazed upon
Show nothing but confusion, eyed awry,
Distinguish form;[3] so your sweet majesty
Looking awry upon your lord's departure,
Finds shapes of grief, more than himself, to wail;
Which, looked on as it is, is nought but shadows
Of what is not:[4] then, thrice-gracious Queen,
More than your lord's departure weep not; more 's not seen;
Or if it be, 't is with false sorrow's eye,
Which, for things true,[5] weeps things imaginary.

QUEEN

It may be so; but yet my inward soul
Persuades me it is otherwise; howe'er it be,
I cannot but be sad; so heavy sad,
As though on thinking on no thought I think,
Makes me with heavy nothing[6] faint and shrink.

BUSHY

'T is nothing but conceit,[7] my gracious lady.

QUEEN

'T is nothing less; conceit is still derived
From some forefather grief; mine is not so,
For nothing hath begot my something grief;
Or something hath the nothing that I grieve;
'T is in reversion that I do possess,[8]
But what it is, that is not yet known, what
I cannot name; 't is nameless woe I wot.[9]

Enter GREEN

10 *well met* – "I am glad to meet you".

11 *is not yet shipped* – "has not yet started".

12 *his designs . . . hope* – "his plans require quick action; his need for quick action (*haste*) makes us hope that he has set off".

13 *our hope, . . . power* – "on whom our hopes of success depend might have brought his men back (*retired his power*)".

14 *strongly . . . land* – "with a strong force (*strongly*) has landed (*set footing*)".

15 *repeals himself . . . arms* – "himself takes off the sentence and bringing an armed force against the king (*with uplifted arms*)".

16 *revolted faction* – "of the rebels (*revolted*) in this conspiracy (*faction*) . . .".

17 *broke his staff* – "broken his staff of office (as steward of the royal household)".

GREEN

God save your majesty, and well met,[10] gentlemen!
I hope the king is not yet shipped[11] for Ireland.

QUEEN

Why hop'st thou so? 'T is better hope he is;
For his designs crave haste, his haste good hope.[12]
Then wherefore dost thou hope he is not shipped?

GREEN

That he, our hope, might have retired his power,[13]
And driven into despair an enemy's hope,
Who strongly hath set footing in this land.[14]
The banished Bolingbroke repeals himself,
And with uplifted arms[15] is safe arrived
At Ravenspurgh.

QUEEN

Now, God in heaven forbid!

GREEN

Oh madam, 't is too true: and that is worse,
The Lord Northumberland, his son young Henry Percy,
The Lords of Ross, Beaumond, and Willoughby,
With all their powerful friends, are fled to him.

BUSHY.

Why have you not proclaimed Northumberland
And all the rest revolted faction,[16] traitors?

GREEN

We have: whereupon the Earl of Worcester
Hath broke his staff,[17] resigned his stewardship,
And all the household servants fled with him
To Bolingbroke.

18 *brought forth . . . mother* – "given birth to her monster (*prodigy*) and I, struggling for breath (*gasping*), a mother who has just given birth to her child . . .". (The queen can now see the reason for her grief which she has compared to an unborn child.)

19 *cozening* – "deceiving".

20 *he is a flatterer . . . extremity* – "that man is a flatterer, one who lives at the expense of others (*parasite*), one who (wrongly) holds back from me my death which otherwise would gently melt away the chains (*bonds*) of this life – a life which unreal hope would make longer (*lingers*) as I lie in pain on my deathbed (*in extremity*)". (The queen welcomes despair as she would welcome death.)

21 *signs of war*, armour.

22 *full of careful . . . looks* – "he looks full of anxiety (*careful*) about his many responsibilities (*business*)".

23 *comfortable* – "comforting".

24 *belie my thoughts* – "be false to what I think".

25 *crosses* – "misfortunes, suffering".

26 *to save* – "to save his Irish kingdom".

QUEEN

So, Green, thou art the midwife to my woe,
And Bolingbroke my sorrow's dismal heir.
Now hath my soul brought forth her prodigy,
And I, a gasping new-delivered mother,[18]
Have woe to woe, sorrow to sorrow joined.

BUSHY

Despair not, madam.

QUEEN

Who shall hinder me?
I will despair, and be at enmity
With cozening[19] hope; he is a flatterer,
A parasite, a keeper-back of death,
Who gently would dissolve the bonds of life,
Which false hope lingers in extremity.[20]

Enter YORK

GREEN

Here comes the Duke of York.

QUEEN

With signs of war[21] about his agéd neck;
Oh, full of careful business are his looks![22]
Uncle, for Heaven's sake, speak comfortable[23] words.

YORK

Should I do so, I should belie my thoughts;[24]
Comfort 's in heaven, and we are on the earth,
Where nothing lives but crosses,[25] care and grief.
Your husband, he is gone to save[26] far off,
Whilst others come to make him lose at home.

27 *to underprop his land* – "to support his kingdom which is ready to fall".

28 *the sick hour that his surfeit made* – "the time when he will, as it were, be sick as a result of his eating too much (*surfeit*)". He will suffer now for wasting so much of his treasure in the past.

29 *try* – "test the worth of".

30 *your son was gone.* Aumerle had gone to join the king in Ireland.

31 *commons cold* – "common people and members of the lower House of Parliament not willing to support the king". (The word *commons* can mean both "the common people" and the "House of Commons".)

32 *my ring* – "my seal ring as a sign that you come from me".

33 *knave* – "boy".

34 *God* – "I pray God . . .".

35 *So my untruth* – "so long as my disloyalty . . .".

36 *with my brother's* – "with Gloucester's".

37 *posts dispatched* – "messengers sent quickly".

Here am I left to underprop his land,[27]
Who, weak with age, cannot support myself.
Now comes the sick hour that his surfeit made;[28]
Now shall he try[29] his friends that flattered him.

Enter a Servant

SERVANT

My lord, your son was gone[30] before I came.

YORK

He was? Why, so; go all which way it will!
The nobles they are fled, the commons cold,[31]
And will, I fear, revolt on Hereford's side.
Sirrah, get thee to Plashy, to my sister Gloucester,
Bid her send me presently a thousand pound.
Hold, take my ring.[32]

SERVANT

My lord, I had forgot to tell your lordship.
Today, as I came by, I calléd there,
But I shall grieve you to report the rest.

YORK

What is 't, knave?[33]

SERVANT

An hour before I came, the duchess died.

YORK

God[34] for his mercy! What a tide of woes
Comes rushing on this woeful land at once!
I know not what to do. I would to God,
So my untruth[35] had not provoked him to it,
The king had cut off my head with my brother's.[36]
What, are there no posts dispatched[37] for Ireland?

38 *If I know . . . hands* – "If I say I know how to control and provide for these affairs, pushed on to me (*thrust into my hands*) in such confusion (*Thus . . . disorderly*) . . .".

39 *Whom conscience . . . right* – "And both my conscience and my relationship to him (*kindred*) tell me that I should help him to get his rights".

40 *somewhat* – "something".

41 *Dispose of you* – "make arrangements for your safety".

42 *uneven* – "in disorder".

43 *at six and seven* – "in confusion".

44 *sits fair* – "goes on (*sits*) blowing strongly (*fair*)".

45 *levy power proportionable to* – "gather as strong a force of soldiers as . . .".

46 *Besides, . . . of those* – "In addition, the closeness (*nearness*) of our friendship (*love*) with the king brings very close to us the hatred of those who . . .".

47 *the wavering commons . . . much* – "the House of Commons, whose members are not firm in loyalty to the king (*wavering*), because their chief love is money and whoever (*whoso*) takes money from them, according to the amount he takes, so he . . .".

How shall we do for money for these wars?
Come, sister – cousin, I would say – pray pardon me.
Go, fellow, get thee home, provide some carts,
And bring away the armour that is there.

[*Exit* Servant

Gentlemen, will you go muster men?
If I know how to order these affairs,
Thus thrust disorderly into my hands,[38]
Never believe me. Both are my kinsmen;
The one is my sovereign, whom both my oath
And duty bids defend: the other again
Is my kinsman, whom the king hath wronged,
Whom conscience, and my kindred bids to right.[39]
Well, somewhat[40] we must do. Come, cousin, I 'll
Dispose of you.[41] Gentlemen, go and muster up your men,
And meet me presently at Berkeley Castle.
I should to Plashy too,
But time will not permit. All is uneven,[42]
And everything is left at six and seven.[43]

[*Exeunt* YORK *and* QUEEN

BUSHY

The wind sits fair[44] for news to go to Ireland,
But none returns. For us to levy power
Proportionable to[45] the enemy,
Is all unpossible.

GREEN

Besides, our nearness to the king in love
Is near the hate of those[46] love not the king.

BAGOT

And that 's the wavering commons, for their love
Lies in their purses, and whoso empties them,
By so much[47] fills their hearts with deadly hate.

48 *Wherein . . . condemned* – "And for this taking of money from them (*Wherein*) the king is very badly thought of (*condemned*) by all (*generally*)".

49 *If judgement . . . so do we* – "If they are judges, then we also shall be condemned to punishment . . .".

50 *little office . . . commons* – "little service the common people and the House of Commons, full of hatred, . . .".

51 *curs* – "worthless dogs".

52 *heart's presages be not vain* – "what my heart knows of the future (*presages*) does not prove untrue (*vain*) . . .".

53 *That 's as York . . . Bolingbroke* – "That depends on how far York is successful in (*thrives to*) driving back Bolingbroke".

54 *numbering sands* – "as impossible as counting the grains of sand on the seashore . . .".

BUSHY

Wherein the king stands generally condemned.[48]

BAGOT

If judgement lie in them, then so do we,[49]
Because we ever have been near the king.

GREEN

Well, I will for refuge straight to Bristol Castle;
The Earl of Wiltshire is already there.

BUSHY

Thither will I with you; for little office
The hateful commons[50] will perform for us,
Except like curs,[51] to tear us all to pieces.
Will you along with us?

BAGOT

No, I 'll to Ireland to his majesty.
Farewell! If heart's presages be not vain,[52]
We three here part that ne'er shall meet again.

BUSHY

That 's as York thrives to beat back Bolingbroke.[53]

GREEN

Alas, poor duke! The task he undertakes
Is numbering sands,[54] and drinking oceans dry;
Where one on his side fights, thousands will fly.
Farewell at once, for once, for all, and ever.

BUSHY

Well, we may meet again.

BAGOT

I fear me, never.

[*Exeunt*

(II.iii) Bolingbroke and Northumberland are riding through Gloucestershire (a county of the west of England) towards Berkeley to meet the Duke of York. Northumberland's son, Harry Percy, overtakes them, bringing news that the Earl of Worcester, Northumberland's brother, has resigned his office as Master of the King's Household, since Northumberland was declared a traitor, and has gone to Ravensburgh to offer his services to Bolingbroke. York has only three hundred men in Berkeley Castle. He sends Lord Berkeley to ask why Bolingbroke, in the absence of the king, has entered England and raised an army. Bolingbroke insists that he must be addressed with the title that was his father's and is now his – Duke, not of Hereford, but of Lancaster. York comes himself from the castle and accuses Bolingbroke of rebellion and treason. Bolingbroke answers very reasonably, reminding his uncle, York, that since he has not been allowed to claim his dukedom through officers of law, he has had to come himself to make the claim; the other nobles speak in his support. York declares that if he had sufficient power he would arrest them all; since he cannot, he will remain neutral, taking the side neither of Bolingbroke nor of Richard. But he invites Bolingbroke and his friends to spend the night in Berkeley Castle, and it is possible, but not certain, that he will go on to Bristol with them on the following day to take prisoner the favourites of the king.

1 *Draws out* – "make longer".
2 *fair discourse* – "pleasing conversation".
3 *bethink me* – "remind myself".
4 *Cotswold*, the Cotswold hills.
5 *wanting* – "lacking, without".
6 *protest . . . travel* – "declare to you has charmed away (*beguiled*) very much of the tiringness (*tediousness*) and length (*process*) of my ride".
7 *But theirs . . . this* – "the others can make their journey pleasant by the hope of seeing Bolingbroke an advantage (*benefit*) I now have; and hoping to be happy (*hope to joy*) is almost as good as being happy (*hope enjoyed*). By looking forward to seeing Bolingbroke. . . ."
8 *whencesoever* – "wherever he is".

Scene III. In Gloucestershire.

Enter BOLINGBROKE *and* NORTHUMBERLAND, *with their* Forces.

BOLINGBROKE

How far is it, my lord, to Berkeley now?

NORTHUMBERLAND

Believe me, noble lord,
I am a stranger here in Gloucestershire;
These high wild hills and rough uneven ways
Draws out[1] our miles, and makes them wearisome.
And yet your fair discourse[2] hath been as sugar,
Making the hard way sweet and delectable.
But I bethink me[3] what a weary way
From Ravenspurgh to Cotswold[4] will be found,
By Ross and Willoughby, wanting[5] your company,
Which, I protest, hath very much beguiled
The tediousness and process of my travel.[6]
But theirs is sweetened with the hope to have
The present benefit which I possess;
And hope to joy is little less, in joy,
Than hope enjoyed. By this,[7] the weary lords
Shall make their way seem short, as mine hath done
By sight of what I have, your noble company.

BOLINGBROKE

Of much less value is my company,
Than your good words. But who comes here?

Enter HARRY PERCY

NORTHUMBERLAND

It is my son, young Harry Percy,
Sent from my brother Worcester, whencesoever.[8]
Harry, how fares your uncle?

9 *forsook* – "left".
10 *o'er by Berkeley* – "across country, through Berkeley . . .".
11 *repair* – "make my way".

PERCY

I had thought, my lord, to have learned his health of you.

NORTHUMBERLAND

Why, is he not with the queen?

PERCY

No, my good lord; he hath forsook[9] the court,
Broken his staff of office and dispersed
The household of the king.

NORTHUMBERLAND

What was his reason?
He was not resolved when last we spake together.

PERCY

Because your lordship was proclaiméd traitor.
But he, my lord, is gone to Ravenspurgh,
To offer service to the Duke of Hereford,
And sent me o'er by Berkeley,[10] to discover
What power the Duke of York had levied there;
Then with directions to repair[11] to Ravenspurgh.

NORTHUMBERLAND

Have you forgot the Duke of Hereford, boy?

PERCY

No, my good lord; for that is not forgot
Which ne'er I did remember: to my knowledge,
I never in my life did look on him.

NORTHUMBERLAND

Then learn to know him now: this is the duke.

12 *tender you my service . . . desert* – "offer (*tender*) you my help for what it is worth, knowing that I am inexperienced (*tender*), unpolished (*raw*) and young, but as I grow older (*elder*) you shall find that I can do more to win your approval and shall deserve more from you". Percy speaks of his service to Bolingbroke as if it is a fruit which will ripen later.

13 *a soul remembering* – "having friends to whom I can be grateful now and generous later".

14 *as my fortune . . . recompense* – "as, with your support (*with thy love*) I come to possess more (*my fortune ripens*), I shall always (*still*) use what I have to reward (*recompense*) your loyalty and help (*true love*)".

15 *thus seals it.* He shakes hands with Percy as if marking the agreement with his seal ring.

16 *what stir Keeps good old York* – "what is York doing to help the king's cause . . .".

17 *of name, and noble estimate* – "of famous name and noble worth (*estimate*)".

18 *Bloody with spurring* – "stained with blood through spurring their horses so hard".

19 *wot . . . recompense* – "know that your friendly support (*love*) follows (*pursues*), or is given to, one who is only a banished traitor; all I have with which to pay you (*my treasury*) is for the present (*yet*) only (*but*) thanks which you cannot feel the value of (*unfelt*); when I have more (*more enriched*) and my thanks are worth more, I shall reward (*recompense*) your friendship (*love*) and your hard work for me (*labour*)".

PERCY

My gracious lord, I tender you my service,
Such as it is, being tender, raw, and young,
Which elder days shall ripen, and confirm
To more approvéd service, and desert.[12]

BOLINGBROKE

I thank thee, gentle Percy, and be sure
I count myself in nothing else so happy
As in a soul remembering[13] my good friends.
And, as my fortune ripens with thy love,
It shall be still thy true love's recompense.[14]
My heart this covenant makes, my hand thus seals it.[15]

NORTHUMBERLAND

How far is it to Berkeley, and what stir
Keeps good old York[16] there, with his men of war?

PERCY

There stands the castle, by yon tuft of trees,
Manned with three hundred men, as I have heard;
And in it are the Lords of York, Berkeley, and Seymour;
None else of name, and noble estimate.[17]

Enter ROSS *and* WILLOUGHBY

NORTHUMBERLAND

Here come the Lords of Ross and Willoughby,
Bloody with spurring,[18] fiery-red with haste.

BOLINGBROKE

Welcome, my lords! I wot your love pursues
A banished traitor; all my treasury
Is yet but unfelt thanks, which more enriched,
Shall be your love and labour's recompense.[19]

20 *surmounts . . . attain it* – "exceeds our hard riding to reach your presence".

21 *Ever more thanks . . . bounty* – "I give you still (*ever*) more thanks – thanks which are like the government money department (*exchequer*) of poor men – and which will have to serve as a substitute (*Stands*) for some generous gift (*bounty*) until my wealth and power (*fortune*) has finished its growing." Bolingbroke speaks of his present wealth as a tiny child (*infant*) which must grow up until it is twenty-one years old (*comes to years*).

22 *to Lancaster* – "since my father's death I am Duke of Lancaster".

23 *Mistake me not* – "Do not misunderstand me".

24 *meaning To raze* – "intention to rub . . .".

25 *absent time . . . arms* – "time of the king's absence and make peaceful England afraid with an army of Englishmen ready for civil war".

ROSS

Your presence makes us rich, most noble lord.

WILLOUGHBY

And far surmounts our labour to attain it.[20]

BOLINGBROKE

Ever more thanks, the exchequer of the poor,
Which till my infant-fortune comes to years,
Stands for my bounty.[21] But who comes here?

Enter BERKELEY

NORTHUMBERLAND

It is my Lord of Berkeley, as I guess.

BERKELEY

My Lord of Hereford, my message is to you.

BOLINGBROKE

My lord, my answer is – to Lancaster;[22]
And I am come to seek that name in England,
And I must find that title in your tongue,
Before I make reply to aught you say.

BERKELEY

Mistake me not,[23] my lord; 't is not my meaning
To raze[24] one title of your honour out.
To you, my lord, I come, what lord you will,
From the most gracious regent of this land,
The Duke of York, to know what pricks you on
To take advantage of the absent time,
And fright our native peace with self-borne arms.[25]

Enter YORK *with* Attendants

26 *transport* – "send".
27 *Whose duty is deceivable* – "whose humble kneeling down (*duty*) is able to deceive".
28 *Tut, tut!* – "Let us stop this nonsense!"
29 *that word grace . . . profane* – "that title of respect, spoken by a person who has no respect for the law (*In an ungracious mouth*), is only (*but*) a wicked misuse of the word".
30 *a dust* – "a grain of dust".
31 *her peaceful bosom . . . despiséd arms?* – "her peaceful land in which they grew up (the word *bosom* suggests that England is their mother and nurse), frightening the villages, so that they turn pale, with the threat of war and a show (*ostentation*) of arms which deserves only to be scorned (*despiséd*)?"
32 *Were I but . . . youth* – "If only (*but*) I were now as full of (*lord of*) the force and courage of youth".
33 *that young Mars of men* – "who seemed, even when a young man, like the god of war (*Mars*) among men of this world".
34 *Now prisoner . . . fault* – "now crippled by the weakness of old age (*palsy*), beat (*chastise*) you down, and give (*minister*) you punishment (*correction*) for your wrongdoing"; (*palsy*, "paralysis, weakness").

the Black Prince, that young Mars of men[33]

BOLINGBROKE

I shall not need transport[26] my words by you;
Here comes his grace in person. My noble uncle!

[*Kneels*

YORK

Show me thy humble heart, and not thy knee,
Whose duty is deceivable,[27] and false.

BOLINGBROKE

My gracious uncle –

YORK

Tut, tut![28]
Grace me no grace, nor uncle me no uncle;
I am no traitor's uncle; and that word grace,
In an ungracious mouth, is but profane.[29]
Why have those banished and forbidden legs
Dared once to touch a dust[30] of England's ground?
But then more "Why?" Why have they dared to march
So many miles upon her peaceful bosom,
Frighting her pale-faced villages with war
And ostentation of despiséd arms?[31]
Com'st thou because the anointed king is hence?
Why, foolish boy, the king is left behind,
And in my loyal bosom lies his power.
Were I but now the lord of such hot youth,[32]
As when brave Gaunt, thy father, and myself
Rescued the Black Prince, that young Mars of men,[33]
From forth the ranks of many thousand French,
Oh then, how quickly should this arm of mine,
Now prisoner to the palsy, chastise thee,
And minister correction to thy fault![34]

35 *let me know . . . wherein* – "tell me what wrong I have done; what kind (*condition*) of wrongdoing is it, and what does it consist of?"

36 *in condition . . . treason* – "of the very worst kind, open and unashamed (*gross*) rebellion and hateful (*detested*) treason".

37 *expiration of thy time* – "end of your sentence".

38 *braving* – "defiant".

39 *indifferent* – "impartial, not favouring either Richard or myself".

40 *stand* – "remain".

41 *royalties . . . Wherefore* – "grants from the king (*royalties*), which I inherited, snatched (*Plucked*) by force (*perforce*) from my coat of arms and given away to wasteful (*unthrifts*) men of low birth who have suddenly risen in the world (*upstart*)? To what position (*Wherefore*) . . .".

42 *trod down* – "oppressed".

43 *To rouse . . . bay* – "to cry out against the injustice and bring it to an end". Bolingbroke speaks as if the injustices were animals to be hunted; *rouse* is "to stir out of hiding"; *chase to the bay* is to hunt the animal until it will turn to fight before it is killed.

44 *denied to sue my livery* – "refused permission (*denied*) to claim possession of my inheritance".

45 *letters patents* – "legal papers of a special kind".

46 *distrained* – "seized by officers of the crown".

47 *amiss employed* – "used for wrong purposes".

48 *challenge law* – "claim my lawful rights".

49 *attorneys are denied me* – "I am refused (*denied*) officers to act for me".

BOLINGBROKE

My gracious uncle, let me know my fault;
On what condition stands it, and wherein?[35]

YORK

Even in condition of the worst degree,
In gross rebellion and detested treason.[36]
Thou art a banished man, and here art come
Before the expiration of thy time,[37]
In braving[38] arms against thy sovereign.

BOLINGBROKE

As I was banished, I was banished Hereford,
But as I come, I come for Lancaster.
And, noble uncle, I beseech your grace
Look on my wrongs with an indifferent[39] eye.
You are my father, for methinks in you
I see old Gaunt alive. Oh then, my father,
Will you permit that I shall stand[40] condemned
A wandering vagabond; my rights and royalties
Plucked from my arms perforce and given away
To upstart unthrifts? Wherefore[41] was I born?
If that my cousin king be King of England,
It must be granted I am Duke of Lancaster.
You have a son, Aumerle, my noble cousin;
Had you first died, and he been thus trod down,[42]
He should have found his uncle Gaunt a father
To rouse his wrongs, and chase them to the bay.[43]
I am denied to sue my livery[44] here,
And yet my letters patents[45] give me leave.
My father's goods are all distrained[46] and sold,
And these and all are all amiss employed.[47]
What would you have me do? I am a subject;
I challenge law:[48] attorneys are denied me;[49]
And therefore personally I lay my claim
To my inheritance of free descent.

50 *abused* – "treated with injustice".

51 *stands . . . right* – "is your responsibility to give him what is just".

52 *Base men . . . great* – "Men of low birth (*Base*) are made rich with the income (*endowments*) which should be Bolingbroke's".

53 *in this kind . . . may not be* – "to come in this way (*kind*), taking up arms in defiance, to help himself and cut his own way forward, to seek for justice (*right*) by breaking the law (*wrong*), it cannot be allowed (*may not be*)". (*Be his own carver* refers to a man cutting himself slices of meat, while *cut out* refers to cutting a pathway.)

54 *for the right of* – "because of the justice of . . .".

55 *joy* – "the joy of heaven".

56 *the issue of these arms* – "what will be the result (*issue*) of your taking up arms".

57 *all ill left* – "badly provided for".

58 *attach . . . mercy* – "arrest (*attach*) you all, and make you submit (*stoop*) to the overriding (*sovereign*) authority of the king, hoping that he might have mercy on your lives".

59 *as neuter* – "as one taking no part in the contest".

NORTHUMBERLAND

The noble duke hath been too much abused.[50]

ROSS

It stands your grace upon to do him right.[51]

WILLOUGHBY

Base men by his endowments are made great.[52]

YORK

My lords of England, let me tell you this:
I have had feeling of my cousin's wrongs,
And laboured all I could to do him right;
But in this kind, to come in braving arms,
Be his own carver, and cut out his way,
To find out right with wrong, it may not be;[53]
And you that do abet him in this kind,
Cherish rebellion, and are rebels all.

NORTHUMBERLAND

The noble duke hath sworn his coming is
But for his own; and for the right of[54] that,
We all have strongly sworn to give him aid,
And let him ne'er see joy[55] that breaks that oath.

YORK

Well, well, I see the issue of these arms.[56]
I cannot mend it, I must needs confess,
Because my power is weak, and all ill left:[57]
But if I could, by Him that gave me life,
I would attach you all, and make you stoop
Unto the sovereign mercy[58] of the king.
But since I cannot, be it known to you,
I do remain as neuter.[59] So, fare you well,
Unless you please to enter in the castle,
And there repose you for this night.

60 *win* – "persuade".

61 *complices . . . commonwealth* – "accomplices, the parasites living on the wealth of the state". (*Caterpillars* live on and spoil the leaves of plants; in Shakespeare's time the word was often used to refer to men who became rich by robbing the government.)

62 *to weed and pluck away*. Bolingbroke now speaks of the caterpillars as if they are themselves the plants, weeds in England's garden which he has sworn to uproot (*pluck away*).

63 *Things past redress . . . care* – "I can no longer have responsibility (*care*) for things which have gone too far (*past*) for me to remedy (*redress*)".

(II.iv) Salisbury, a supporter of King Richard, is told by a leader of a great army of Welshmen that the men are now going back to their homes. No news has come from the king and they believe that he is dead.

1 *hardly* – "with difficulty".

2 *bay-trees* – "laurels". A crown of laurel wreaths was given as a sign of victory, so that the fact that the leaves of these trees had begun to die was looked on as a sign of approaching defeat.

3 *meteors*. Falling stars (which, the Captain says, seemed to frighten even those stars which have an unchanging place) are also thought of as a sign of misfortune to come.

BOLINGBROKE

An offer, uncle, that we will accept:
But we must win[60] your grace to go with us
To Bristol Castle, which they say is held
By Bushy, Bagot, and their complices,
The caterpillars of the commonwealth,[61]
Which I have sworn to weed and pluck away.[62]

YORK

It may be I will go with you: but yet I 'll pause,
For I am loath to break our country's laws.
Nor friends, nor foes, to me welcome you are;
Things past redress are now with me past care.[63]

[*Exeunt*

Scene IV. A camp in Wales.

Enter SALISBURY *and a* Welsh Captain.

CAPTAIN

My Lord of Salisbury, we have stayed ten days,
And hardly[1] kept our countrymen together,
And yet we hear no tidings from the king.
Therefore we will disperse ourselves; farewell!

SALISBURY

Stay yet another day, thou trusty Welshman;
The king reposeth all his confidence in thee.

CAPTAIN

'T is thought the king is dead; we will not stay.
The bay-trees[2] in our country are all withered,
And meteors[3] fright the fixéd stars of heaven;
The pale-faced moon looks bloody on the earth,

4 *lean-looked* – "thin-looking".
5 *The other to enjoy by rage* – "the others in hope of what they may get by violence (*rage*) . . .".
6 *forerun* – "are seen before . . .".
7 *As well assured* – "because they feel certain . . .".
8 *heavy mind* – "one who feels sorrow".
9 *like a shooting star*. Richard's power (*glory*) also is falling, like a falling star, from the sky (*firmament*) to the earth below (*base*). His time of success is like a setting sun in a rainy (*weeping*) sky, a sign of (*Witnessing*) future storms.
10 *wait upon* – "join".
11 *crossly . . . goes* – "all good luck (*fortune*) is going to the other side"; (*crossly*, "contrary, opposite").

And lean-looked[4] prophets whisper fearful change;
Rich men look sad, and ruffians dance and leap,
The one in fear, to lose what they enjoy,
The other to enjoy by rage,[5] and war.
These signs forerun[6] the death or fall of kings.
Farewell! Our countrymen are gone and fled,
As well assured[7] Richard, their king, is dead.

[*Exit*

SALISBURY

Ah, Richard, with the eyes of heavy mind,[8]
I see thy glory, like a shooting star,[9]
Fall to the base earth from the firmament.
Thy sun sets weeping in the lowly west,
Witnessing storms to come, woe, and unrest.
Thy friends are fled to wait upon[10] thy foes,
And crossly to thy good all fortune goes.[11]

[*Exit*

(III.i) Outside Bristol Castle, Bolingbroke, now assuming authority, sends to execution Bushy and Green, the king's favourites whom he has taken prisoner; he charges them with having misled King Richard, brought sorrow to the queen, and with having persuaded the king that he (Bolingbroke) was the king's enemy. So he has been banished while they have taken his inheritance. It is worth noticing that the Duke of York has come to Bristol with Bolingbroke.

1 *part your bodies . . . charity* – "part from your bodies – by speaking at length with too much force about your wicked lives, for that would be (*were*) no kindness (*charity*)".

2 *to wash your blood . . . hands* – "to clear myself of the guilt of your execution".

3 *unfold* – "make known".

4 *A happy gentleman . . . manner* – "a gentleman fortunate in family (*blood*) and appearance (*lineaments*), made unhappy and completely (*clean*) spoilt (*disfigured*) by you: you have, as one may say, . . .".

5 *in blood . . . love* – "in family relationship, and near in friendship . . .".

6 *stooped my neck under your injuries* – "had to submit to the injuries you did me".

7 *in foreign clouds . . . signories* – "into clouds in foreign lands, feeling sorrow with every moment (at every mouthful of bread); while you have grown fat, or rich, with my estates (*signories*)".

8 *Disparked* – "made into common land".

9 *torn my household coat . . . impress* – "knocked out my family coat of arms which was painted on the glass, rubbed out my family crest".

10 *Save men's opinions . . . blood* – "except (*Save*) men's opinions of me, and the fact that I am still alive . . .".

ACT THREE

Scene I. Bristol. Outside the Castle.

Enter BOLINGBROKE, YORK, NORTHUMBERLAND, ROSS, PERCY, WILLOUGHBY, *with* BUSHY *and* GREEN, *prisoners.*

BOLINGBROKE

Bring forth these men.
Bushy and Green, I will not vex your souls –
Since presently your souls must part your bodies –
With too much urging your pernicious lives,
For 't were no charity;[1] yet, to wash your blood
From off my hands,[2] here in the view of men,
I will unfold[3] some causes of your deaths.
You have misled a prince, a royal king,
A happy gentleman in blood and lineaments,
By you unhappied, and disfigured clean:
You have in manner[4] with your sinful hours
Made a divorce betwixt his queen and him,
Broke the possession of a royal bed,
And stained the beauty of a fair queen's cheeks
With tears drawn from her eyes by your foul wrongs.
Myself, a prince by fortune of my birth,
Near to the king in blood, and near in love,[5]
Till you did make him misinterpret me,
Have stooped my neck under your injuries,[6]
And sighed my English breath in foreign clouds,
Eating the bitter bread of banishment;
Whilst you have fed upon my signories,[7]
Disparked[8] my parks and felled my forest woods,
From my own windows torn my household coat,
Razed out my impress,[9] leaving me no sign,
Save men's opinions, and my living blood,[10]

11 *of death*, by the executioner's axe.
12 *plague injustice* – "punish those who have done us this wrong . . .".
13 *dispatched* – "sent to their death".
14 *fairly . . . entreated* – "let her be treated well".
15 *commends* – "greetings, good wishes".
16 *dispatched . . . large* – "sent with letters telling at length (*large*) of your kind feelings towards her".
17 *complices* – "fellow-conspirators".

See them delivered over
To execution and the hand of death[11]

To show the world I am a gentleman.
This, and much more, much more than twice all this,
Condemns you to the death. See them delivered over
To execution and the hand of death.[11]

BUSHY

More welcome is the stroke of death to me,
Than Bolingbroke to England. Lords, farewell!

GREEN

My comfort is that heaven will take our souls
And plague injustice[12] with the pains of hell.

BOLINGBROKE

My Lord Northumberland, see them dispatched.[13]
[*Exeunt* NORTHUMBERLAND *and* others *with the* prisoners
Uncle, you say the queen is at your house.
For God's sake, fairly let her be entreated,[14]
Tell her I send to her my kind commends;[15]
Take special care my greetings be delivered.

YORK

A gentleman of mine I have dispatched
With letters of your love to her at large.[16]

BOLINGBROKE

Thanks, gentle uncle: come, lords, away,
To fight with Glendower and his complices;[17]
Awhile to work, and after holiday!

[*Exeunt*

(III.ii) Richard has landed on the Welsh coast near the castle of Barkloughly (not, it should be remembered, the Berkeley, in Gloucestershire, where Bolingbroke met York). He greets his kingdom's earth with smiles and tears, begging it to bring death to his enemies. Carlisle and Aumerle remind him that they must take action against Bolingbroke, but Richard is confident that the rebellion will end now that the true king has come back. Salisbury tells him that he has come back a day too late; the army of twelve thousand Welshmen has scattered or joined with Bolingbroke, believing that Richard was dead. Richard turns pale at this. Scroop brings the news that everyone is supporting the side of Bolingbroke, even old men, young boys and women. The king asks angrily what his favourites have been doing. Why have they allowed Bolingbroke to come so far into England? When he is told that they have been put to death, he begins to think of his own death – all he has belongs now to Bolingbroke. Carlisle reminds him that a brave man must fight; Aumerle suggests that he should ask where the Duke of York is and what forces he has. Scroop tells them that York has joined Bolingbroke; the castles of the north of England have surrendered and the nobles of the south are on Bolingbroke's side. Richard will hear no more of comfort or advice. He discharges his army and goes to Flint Castle.

1 *brooks* – "enjoys".
2 *As a long-parted . . . meeting* – "as a mother who has been separated (*parted*) for a long time from her child, foolishly (*fondly*) mixes tears and smiles when she meets the child again . . .".
3 *do thee favours* – "touch you lovingly".
4 *heavy-gaited* – "slow-moving".
5 *annoyance* – "harm, injury". Spiders and toads were believed to give off poison.
6 *Guard it* – "let it be accompanied . . .".
7 *double . . . throw* – "forked (*double*) tongue may, with deadly (*mortal*) touch, send out . . .".
8 *senseless conjuration* – "my calling on (*conjuration*) the earth which cannot hear me (*senseless*)".
9 *under foul rebellion's arms* – "under the attack of evil (*foul*) armed rebels".

Scene II. The coast of Wales. A castle in sight.

Drums: flourish and colours. Enter RICHARD, AUMERLE, *the* BISHOP OF CARLISLE, *and* Soldiers.

KING RICHARD

Barkloughly Castle call they this at hand?

AUMERLE

Yea, my lord: how brooks[1] your grace the air,
After your late tossing on the breaking seas?

KING RICHARD

Needs must I like it well: I weep for joy
To stand upon my kingdom once again.
Dear earth, I do salute thee with my hand,
Though rebels wound thee with their horses' hoofs;
As a long-parted mother, with her child,
Plays fondly with her tears and smiles in meeting,[2]
So weeping, smiling, greet I thee, my earth,
And do thee favours[3] with my royal hands.
Feed not thy sovereign's foe, my gentle earth,
Nor with thy sweets comfort his ravenous sense;
But let thy spiders, that suck up thy venom,
And heavy-gaited[4] toads lie in their way,
Doing annoyance[5] to the treacherous feet,
Which with usurping steps do trample thee.
Yield stinging nettles to mine enemies;
And when they from thy bosom pluck a flower,
Guard it,[6] I pray thee, with a lurking adder,
Whose double tongue may with a mortal touch
Throw[7] death upon thy sovereign's enemies.
Mock not my senseless conjuration,[8] lords;
This earth shall have a feeling, and these stones
Prove armèd soldiers, ere her native king
Shall falter under foul rebellion's arms.[9]

10 *That power*, of God, the "divine right" of kings.

11 *embracéd* – "seized, used to the full".

12 *else, if heaven . . . will not* – "otherwise, if God would like to help us, and we will not help ourselves . . .".

13 *The proffered means . . . redress* – "the opportunity (*means*) of help (*succour*) and remedy (*redress*) which God sets before us (*proffered*)".

14 *security* – "over-confidence".

15 *in substance and in power* – "in possessions and authority".

16 *Discomfortable* – "Discouraging".

17 *the searching eye . . . world* – "the sun (*eye of heaven*), which lights this earth (*lower world*) and sees everything (*searching*), is hidden from us and shining on the other side (*Behind*) of the globe . . .".

18 *range abroad* – "move freely about".

19 *He fires* – "the sun shines like fire on . . .".

20 *every guilty hole* – "every hiding-place of a guilty person".

21 *murders . . . themselves* – "those who are guilty of murder, treason and other hateful (*detested*) crimes, no longer hidden in the darkness of night, are seen and known for what they are (*Stand bare and naked*), and they themselves are afraid (*trembling*) at what they have done (*at themselves*)"; (*cloak*, a loose-fitting garment which can be wrapped round so that the person inside is hidden).

22 *hath revelled . . . self-affrighted* – "has enjoyed full freedom (*hath revelled*) in the night, while the sun was on its journey (*wandering*) over the part of the world opposite to England (*Antipodes*) (i.e. while the sun of England, its king, was absent), shall see the king on his throne like the sun rising in the east, then Bolingbroke will be ashamed of his treason (*His treasons will sit blushing in his face*), full of fear of what the king will do (*Not able to endure the sight of day*), and afraid even of his own crimes (*self-affrighted*)".

23 *balm* – "sweet oil". Nothing can take away from a king the power that God has given him when he is sprinkled with holy oil (*anointed*) as he is crowned.

CARLISLE

Fear not, my lord! That power[10] that made you king
Hath power to keep you king. In spite of all,
The means that heaven yields must be embracéd[11]
And not neglected; else, if heaven would,
And we will not,[12] heaven's offer we refuse,
The proffered means of succour and redress.[13]

AUMERLE

He means, my lord, that we are too remiss,
Whilst Bolingbroke, through our security,[14]
Grows strong and great in substance and in power.[15]

KING RICHARD

Discomfortable[16] cousin, know'st thou not
That, when the searching eye of heaven is hid
Behind the globe, that lights the lower world,[17]
Then thieves and robbers range abroad[18] unseen,
In murders and in outrage bloody here:
But when from under this terrestrial ball,
He fires[19] the proud tops of the eastern pines,
And darts his light through every guilty hole,[20]
Then murders, treasons, and detested sins,
The cloak of night being plucked from off their backs,
Stand bare and naked, trembling at themselves.[21]
So when this thief, this traitor, Bolingbroke,
Who all this while hath revelled in the night,
Whilst we were wandering with the Antipodes,
Shall see us rising in our throne, the east,
His treasons will sit blushing in his face,
Not able to endure the sight of day,
But self-affrighted[22] tremble at his sin.
Not all the water in the rough rude sea
Can wash the balm[23] from an anointed king.

24 *The breath . . . elected* – "No voice (*breath*) of men of this world (*worldly*) can put off his throne (*depose*) the substitute (*deputy*) for Himself, chosen (*elected*) . . .".

25 *pressed To lift shrewd steel* – "forced into his army (*pressed*) to lift a sharp (*shrewd*) weapon . . .".

26 *in heavenly pay* – "serving for his wages on the side of heaven". (Richard is using the word *angel* with two meanings; "a spirit of God" and "a golden coin, worth about ten shillings".)

27 *Nor near* – "Neither nearer . . .".

28 *Discomfort guides my tongue* – "Want of hope (*Discomfort*) prompts my words".

29 *clouded* – "hidden the sunshine, spoilt the good fortune of . . .".

30 *O'erthrows thy joys* – "destroys your happiness".

31 *Comfort* – "Do not be discouraged".

32 *But now* – "A moment ago . . ."

33 *Did triumph in* – "gave confidence and colour to".

34 *time hath set . . . pride* – "the present time (my coming a day too late) has brought disgrace (*a blot*) upon me as a king".

The breath of worldly men cannot depose
The deputy elected[24] by the Lord.
For every man that Bolingbroke hath pressed
To lift shrewd steel[25] against our golden crown,
God, for his Richard, hath in heavenly pay[26]
A glorious angel: then, if angels fight,
Weak men must fall, for heaven still guards the right.

Enter SALISBURY

Welcome, my lord! How far off lies your power?

SALISBURY

Nor near[27] nor farther off, my gracious lord,
Than this weak arm. Discomfort guides my tongue,[28]
And bids me speak of nothing but despair.
One day too late, I fear me, noble lord,
Hath clouded[29] all thy happy days on earth.
Oh, call back yesterday, bid time return,
And thou shalt have twelve thousand fighting men!
Today, today, unhappy day, too late,
O'erthrows thy joys,[30] friends, fortune, and thy state;
For all the Welshmen, hearing thou wert dead,
Are gone to Bolingbroke, dispersed, and fled.

AUMERLE

Comfort,[31] my liege! Why looks your grace so pale?

KING RICHARD

But now[32] the blood of twenty thousand men
Did triumph in[33] my face, and they are fled;
And till so much blood thither come again,
Have I not reason to look pale, and dead?
All souls that will be safe, fly from my side,
For time hath set a blot upon my pride.[34]

35 *High* – "Noble, ambitious".
36 *to serve our turn* – "for our needs".
37 *betide . . . him* – "come to my lord than my words, chosen (*-tuned*) to fit my sorrowful news (*care-*), can announce (*deliver*) to him".
38 *is worldly loss . . . unfold* – "that you can make known (*unfold*) is loss in this world".
39 *'t was my care* – "looking after it caused me great trouble".
40 *Cry* – "if you announce the news of . . .".

Thy very beadsmen learn to bend their bows

AUMERLE

Comfort, my liege; remember who you are.

KING RICHARD

I had forgot myself. Am I not king?
Awake, thou coward majesty! Thou sleep'st.
Is not the king's name twenty thousand names?
Arm, arm, my name! A puny subject strikes
At thy great glory. Look not to the ground,
Ye favourites of a king; are we not high?
High[35] be our thoughts! I know my uncle York
Hath power enough to serve our turn.[36]
But who comes here?

Enter SCROOP

SCROOP

More health and happiness betide my liege
Than can my care-tuned tongue deliver him![37]

KING RICHARD

Mine ear is open, and my heart prepared.
The worst is worldly loss thou canst unfold.[38]
Say, is my kingdom lost? Why, 't was my care;[39]
And what loss is it to be rid of care?
Strives Bolingbroke to be as great as we?
Greater he shall not be: if he serve God,
We 'll serve him too, and be his fellow so.
Revolt our subjects? That we cannot mend.
They break their faith to God, as well as us:
Cry[40] woe, destruction, ruin, loss, decay,
The worst is death, and death will have his day.

41 *Like an unseasonable . . . bright steel* – "As a storm at the wrong time (*unseasonable*) may cause a flood, as if the world had all melted (*dissolved*) to tears, so the angry power (*rage*) of Bolingbroke, (at the wrong time, when you were in Ireland), has grown (*swells*) like a river bursting its banks (*So high above his limits*), and covers your land, which is full of fear, not with silver river water, but with cruel (*hard*) and shining (*bright*) weapons (*steel*) . . .".

42 *White beards . . . arms* – "Even the old men with silver beards, thin hair or bald heads (*hairless scalps*) have put on helmets to fight against you; boys whose voices have not yet broken (*with women's voices*) try to speak bravely and like men (*big*), and fasten (*clap*) armour (*arms*), which is too hard (*stiff*) and difficult for them to manage (*unwieldy*) on to their girlish limbs (*joints*)".

43 *Thy very beadsmen . . . yew* – "even the old men whose only duty is to say prayers for you (*beadsmen*) are learning to shoot arrows from their bows of yew, so that the yew tree (which, because it has poisonous berries, is an emblem of death) becomes deadly for a second reason (*double-fatal*)".

44 *Yea, . . . bills* – "yes, even women who were spinning at their distaffs learn instead to handle old bills"; (*distaff*, "the stick from which the wool is pulled". *bill*, "weapon in the form of a blade fixed to a long wooden handle").

45 *Measure our confines . . . steps* – "make their stately way (*Measure*) within the boundaries (*confines*) of my land unopposed (*with such peaceful steps*)".

46 *warrant* – "am quite sure (dare to give a pledge that it is true)".

47 *vipers.* Vipers (poisonous snakes) were thought to be treacherous.

distaff-women

SCROOP

Glad am I that your highness is so armed
To bear the tidings of calamity.
Like an unseasonable stormy day,
Which makes the silver rivers drown their shores,
As if the world were all dissolved to tears,
So high above his limits, swells the rage
Of Bolingbroke, covering your fearful land
With hard bright steel,[41] and hearts harder than steel.
White beards have armed their thin and hairless scalps
Against thy majesty, and boys with women's voices
Strive to speak big, and clap their female joints
In stiff unwieldy arms;[42] against thy crown
Thy very beadsmen learn to bend their bows
Of double-fatal yew:[43] against thy state,
Yea, distaff-women manage rusty bills.[44]
Against thy seat both young and old rebel,
And all goes worse than I have power to tell.

KING RICHARD

Too well, too well thou tell'st a tale so ill.
Where is the Earl of Wiltshire? Where is Bagot?
What is become of Bushy, where is Green
That they have let the dangerous enemy
Measure our confines with such peaceful steps?[45]
If we prevail, their heads shall pay for it.
I warrant[46] they have made peace with Bolingbroke.

SCROOP

Peace have they made with him indeed, my lord.

KING RICHARD

O villains, vipers,[47] damned without redemption!
Dogs easily won to fawn on any man!
Snakes in my heart-blood warmed, that sting my heart!

48 *Judas*, the follower of Christ who betrayed him.
49 *spotted*, as snakes are, and also with their sin of treachery.
50 *his property* – "its characteristic".
51 *hands* – "shaking hands with Bolingbroke".
52 *graved . . . ground* – "buried (*graved*) in their graves dug in the earth"; (*hollow*, "to dig out a hole").
53 *Make dust . . . earth* – "using the dusty earth as our paper and our tears as ink to write words of sorrow (on my grave)".
54 *Save* – "except".
55 *model of the barren earth* – "shape modelled out of unfruitful (*barren*) dust".

Three Judases, each one thrice worse than Judas![48]
Would they make peace? Terrible hell make war
Upon their spotted[49] souls for this offence!

SCROOP

Sweet love, I see, changing his property,[50]
Turns to the sourest, and most deadly hate.
Again uncurse their souls; their peace is made
With heads, and not with hands![51] Those whom you curse
Have felt the worst of death's destroying wound,
And lie full low, graved in the hollow ground.[52]

AUMERLE

Is Bushy, Green and the Earl of Wiltshire dead?

SCROOP

Ay, all of them at Bristol lost their heads.

AUMERLE

Where is the duke, my father, with his power?

KING RICHARD

No matter where; of comfort no man speak.
Let 's talk of graves, of worms, and epitaphs,
Make dust our paper, and with rainy eyes
Write sorrow on the bosom of the earth.[53]
Let 's choose executors, and talk of wills;
And yet not so; for what can we bequeath,
Save[54] our deposéd bodies to the ground?
Our lands, our lives, and all are Bolingbroke's,
And nothing can we call our own but death,
And that small model of the barren earth,[55]
Which serves as paste and cover to our bones.

56 *within the hollow crown . . . sits* – "inside (*within*) this hollow crown which encircles (*rounds*) the forehead (*temples*) of a king who must one day die (*mortal*), it seems as if there is another king, Death, who sits there imitating the real king in an amusing and scornful way"; (*hollow* suggests that just as a king's crown is not solid, so his splendid power cannot last; *antic*, "clown, a man who amuses people by acting in a foolish way").

57 *Scoffing his state* – "mocking at (*Scoffing*) the king's (*his*) splendid way of living (*state*)".

58 *a breath . . . To monarchise* – "a tiny moment of life (*breath*), a very short scene to take part in on life's stage, to act like a king (*monarchise*) . . .".

59 *Infusing him . . . conceit* – "filling (*Infusing*) him with pride in his own power (*self*), a pride which is nothing but empty (*vain*) imagination"; (*conceit* has two meanings here, "pride" and "imagination").

60 *flesh . . . and with* – "flesh and blood, which surrounds and guards our human life like a castle wall (*walls*), were made out of brass and and able to be defended against all attacks (*impregnable*); and when the king has been led gently on (*humoured*) to believe this (*thus*), Death comes in the end (*at the last*) and with no more than . . .".

61 *Cover your heads* – "Put on your hats". They are standing bareheaded in the king's presence.

62 *form* – "formal court behaviour".

63 *but mistook . . . while* – "only (*but*) been mistaken about me all this time (*while*)".

64 *Subjected thus* – "Controlled by these needs".

65 *presently . . . to wail* – "at once (*presently*) put an end in advance to (*prevent*) every reason (*ways*) for crying out in grief (*to wail*)".

66 *oppresseth strength . . . follies* – "pulls down and defeats your power and energy, adds to the power of your enemy by making you weaker (*in your weakness*), so that your foolish fears (*follies*) . . .".

67 *Fear and be slain . . . breath* – "No weaker (*worse*) man can come to battle than one who is afraid and is killed because of his fear; to fight bravely and to die is to destroy the power of death and to win fame by one's own courage in dying, whereas (*where*) to be afraid of dying is like paying Death with words (*breath*) of flattery, as a slave (*servile*), for every day he lets you live".

For God's sake, let us sit upon the ground,
And tell sad stories of the death of kings;
How some have been deposed, some slain in war,
Some haunted by the ghosts they have deposed,
Some poisoned by their wives, some sleeping killed,
All murdered. For within the hollow crown
That rounds the mortal temples of a king,
Keeps death his court, and there the antic sits,[56]
Scoffing his state[57] and grinning at his pomp,
Allowing him a breath, a little scene,
To monarchise,[58] be feared, and kill with looks,
Infusing him with self and vain conceit,[59]
As if this flesh, which walls about our life,
Were brass impregnable; and humoured thus,
Comes at the last, and, with[60] a little pin,
Bores through his castle wall, and farewell king!
Cover your heads[61] and mock not flesh and blood
With solemn reverence; throw away respect,
Tradition, form,[62] and ceremonious duty,
For you have but mistook me all this while.[63]
I live with bread like you, feel want,
Taste grief, need friends. Subjected thus,[64]
How can you say to me, I am a king?

CARLISLE

My lord, wise men ne'er sit and wail their woes,
But presently prevent the ways to wail.[65]
To fear the foe, since fear oppresseth strength,
Gives, in your weakness, strength unto your foe,
And so your follies[66] fight against yourself.
Fear and be slain, no worse can come to fight;
And fight and die is death destroying death,
Where fearing dying pays death servile breath.[67]

68 *power . . . limb* – "band of soldiers; find out where he is and let us try to make the most of the little we have".

69 *change blows . . . over-blown* – "exchange blows with you to see which of us is fated to die. My fears, which were like a fit of shivering fever (*ague*), have blown away (*over* –)".

70 *lies* – "is stationed".

71 *complexion . . . day* – "look (*complexion*) of the sky what the weather is (*state*) and what it is going to be (*inclination*)".

72 *by small and small* – "little by little".

73 *yielded up* – "surrendered".

74 *Beshrew thee . . . despair* – "May sorrow come upon you (*Beshrew thee*), cousin, for encouraging me to hope again when I was ready to give up all hope and so to suffer no more". Richard was on the pleasant path (*sweet way*) to hopelessness when Aumerle led him away to another road.

AUMERLE

My father hath a power; inquire of him,
And learn to make a body of a limb.[68]

KING RICHARD

Thou chid'st me well! Proud Bolingbroke, I come
To change blows with thee, for our day of doom!
This ague fit of fear is over-blown;[69]
An easy task it is to win our own.
Say Scroop, where lies[70] our uncle with his power?
Speak sweetly, man, although thy looks be sour.

SCROOP

Men judge by the complexion of the sky
The state and inclination of the day;[71]
So may you by my dull and heavy eye.
My tongue hath but a heavier tale to say:
I play the torturer, by small and small[72]
To lengthen out the worst that must be spoken.
Your uncle York is joined with Bolingbroke,
And all your northern castles yielded up,[73]
And all your southern gentlemen in arms
Upon his faction.

KING RICHARD

Thou hast said enough.
[*To* AUMERLE] Beshrew thee, cousin, which didst lead me forth
Of that sweet way I was in to despair:[74]
What say you now? What comfort have we now?
By heaven, I'll hate him everlastingly,
That bids me be of comfort any more.
Go to Flint Castle; there I'll pine away;
A king, woe's slave, shall kingly woe obey.
That power I have, discharge; and let them go

75 *ear* – "plough and sow".
76 *counsel is but vain* – "giving advice is only a waste of words".
77 *double wrong*, in thinking that he can deceive me and in causing me more grief by trying to make me hope again.

(III.iii) Bolingbroke's forces have come to Flint Castle. They hear that King Richard is there. Bolingbroke sends a message to the king asking that he may be allowed to return from banishment and have his lands given back; if not, he must lead his forces to battle. King Richard appears on the castle walls: he is angry that Bolingbroke's messenger, Northumberland, does not kneel before him and speaks of the power of God to punish any who attack the king. Northumberland gives the message and Richard accepts Bolingbroke's conditions. He asks Aumerle would it not be better to refuse and die at once. As Northumberland returns he wonders if he must now be deposed; will King Bolingbroke allow him to live out his life? He comes down into the courtyard at Bolingbroke's request and Bolingbroke kneels before him with courteous words. Bolingbroke still pretends that he has come only for his dukedom but, as they set out for London, Richard knows that all power is now in Bolingbroke's hands.

1 *colours* – "flags".
2 *beseem* – "be more seemly, more proper for . . .".
3 *should* – "should have to".

To ear[75] the land that hath some hope to grow,
For I have none. Let no man speak again
To alter this, for counsel is but vain.[76]

AUMERLE

My liege, one word.

KING RICHARD

He does me double wrong,[77]
That wounds me with the flatteries of his tongue.
Discharge my followers: let them hence away,
From Richard's night to Bolingbroke's fair day.

[*Exeunt*

Scene III. Wales. Outside Flint Castle.

Enter with drum and colours,[1] BOLINGBROKE, YORK, NORTHUMBERLAND, Attendants *and* forces.

BOLINGBROKE

So that by this intelligence we learn
The Welshmen are dispersed, and Salisbury
Is gone to meet the king, who lately landed
With some few private friends, upon this coast.

NORTHUMBERLAND

The news is very fair and good, my lord:
Richard not far from hence hath hid his head.

YORK

It would beseem[2] the Lord Northumberland,
To say "King Richard". Alack, the heavy day,
When such a sacred king should[3] hide his head!

4 *to shorten you . . . length* – "as to cut off your head for so cutting off (*taking*) his title as king (*head*)".

5 *Mistake not, uncle . . . should* – "Do not make too much of your misunderstanding of what Northumberland meant".

6 *Lest you mistake . . . heads* – "for fear (*Lest*) you forget, in wrongly taking power, that God is watching from above"; (*mistake* is used in two meanings, "to understand wrongly," i.e. "to forget", and "to take unjustly").

7 *oppose not myself . . . will.* Bolingbroke believes that it may be the will of God that he should take power.

8 *The castle . . . entrance* – "The king is among those who are holding this castle against you".

NORTHUMBERLAND

Your grace mistakes; only to be brief,
Left I his title out.

YORK

The time hath been,
Would you have been so brief with him, he would
Have been so brief with you, to shorten you,
For taking so the head, your whole head's length.[4]

BOLINGBROKE

Mistake not, uncle, farther than you should.[5]

YORK

Take not, good cousin, farther than you should,
Lest you mistake the heavens are o'er our heads.[6]

BOLINGBROKE

I know it, uncle, and oppose not myself
Against their will.[7] But who comes here?

Enter PERCY

Welcome, Harry. What, will not this castle yield?

PERCY

The castle royally is manned, my lord,
Against thy entrance.[8]

BOLINGBROKE

Royally?
Why, it contains no king?

9 *lies* – "is living or lodging".
10 *belike* – "very likely".
11 *rude ribs* – "rough walls" (as a man's ribs form the walls of his chest).
12 *breath of parley* – "sound which calls for a truce (*parley*)".
13 *Provided that . . . granted* – "on condition (*Provided*) that my recall from banishment (*banishment repealed*) and the restoration of my estates is willingly (*freely*) granted".
14 *the advantage of my power* – "the fact that my power is stronger".
15 *lay the summer's dust.* Bolingbroke might bring about a civil war in which blood would fall like rain to lay the dust which rises from the ground in summer; that he does not wish for such a storm (*tempest*) of blood-red rain to soak (*bedrench*) England's green grass will be shown when he kneels before the king (*My stooping duty*).
16 *signify as much* – "and say words which mean (*signify*) this".
17 *tattered battlements . . . perused* – "half-ruined walls they may clearly see the loyal promises and conditions which I am offering, as well as the splendid equipment which we have"; (*tattered*, "ragged"; *appointment* probably has two meanings here, "promise, condition" and "equipment"; *peruse*, "to see, read").

this castle's tattered battlements

PERCY

Yes, my good lord,
It doth contain a king: King Richard lies[9]
Within the limits of yon lime and stone,
And with him are the Lord Aumerle, Lord Salisbury,
Sir Stephen Scroop, besides a clergyman
Of holy reverence; who, I cannot learn.

NORTHUMBERLAND

Oh, belike[10] it is the Bishop of Carlisle.

BOLINGBROKE

Noble lords,
Go to the rude ribs[11] of that ancient castle,
Through brazen trumpet send the breath of parley[12]
Into his ruined ears, and thus deliver:
Henry Bolingbroke
On both his knees doth kiss King Richard's hand
And sends allegiance and true faith of heart
To his most royal person: hither come
Even at his feet to lay my arms and power,
Provided that my banishment repealed
And lands restored again, be freely granted:[13]
If not, I 'll use the advantage of my power[14]
And lay the summer's dust[15] with showers of blood,
Rained from the wounds of slaughtered Englishmen;
The which, how far off from the mind of Bolingbroke
It is, such crimson tempest should bedrench
The fresh green lap of fair King Richard's land,
My stooping duty tenderly shall show.
Go, signify as much,[16] while here we march
Upon the grassy carpet of this plain,
Let 's march without the noise of threatening drum,
That from this castle's tattered battlements
Our fair appointments may be well perused.[17]

18 *Methinks . . . fire* – "It seems to me (*Methinks*) that the meeting between King Richard and myself should be as full of fear (*terror*) – for the onlookers – as when lightning and rain, (*the elements Of fire and water*) seem to attack each other, and the clouds which cover the face (*the cloudy cheeks*) of the sky are torn by the thunder of their battle (*thundering shock*). Let King Richard be the fiery lightning . . .".

19 *The rage be his . . . on him* – "Let him be full of anger (*rage*), while I drop tears of sorrow on the ground; Richard himself I will not touch".

20 *Parley . . . within* – "The trumpet note for a truce (*Parley*) is sounded on the stage (*without*), and an answering sound is heard from a room behind (*within*)".

21 *on the walls*, on the balcony over the back of the stage, as if on the walls of the castle.

22 *the blushing discontented sun* – "the sun flushed with anger".

23 *portal* – "gateway".

24 *the envious clouds . . . occident.* A red sky when the sun rises is believed to be a sign of stormy weather. Richard is red with anger when he sees Bolingbroke, just as the sun is red in the eastern sky when it sees that the jealous (*envious*) clouds are intending (*bent*) to darken its splendid path (*track*) to the west (*occident*).

25 *eagle's.* The eagle, king of birds, was spoken of in proverbs as having clear and strong sight.

26 *lightens forth . . . show* – "seems to send out (*forth*) flashes of lightning which show the power of a king (*majesty*) to make everyone obey (*Controlling*). Oh (*Alack*), how sorry I am (*for woe*) that anything (done by Richard himself or by Bolingbroke) should hurt (*harm*) or spoil (*stain*) the splendid (*fair*) appearance (*show*) of such a man!"

27 *To watch . . . knee* – "waiting to see (*watch*) you kneel down in fear before me". Northumberland does not show this usual sign of respect.

28 *To pay . . . presence* – "to carry out the duty they owe of showing fear and respect (*awful*) to me".

29 *the hand of God.* Richard believes that only God can dismiss him from his throne which he holds as God's officer.

30 *gripe* – "grasp, take hold of".

Methinks King Richard and myself should meet
With no less terror than the elements
Of fire and water, when their thundering shock
At meeting tears the cloudy cheeks of heaven:
Be he the fire,[18] I 'll be the yielding water;
The rage be his, whilst on the earth I rain
My waters; on the earth, and not on him.[19]
March on, and mark King Richard, how he looks.

Parley without, and answer within.[20] *Then a flourish.*
Enter on the walls,[21] KING RICHARD, CARLISLE, AUMERLE, SCROOP *and* SALISBURY

See, see, King Richard doth himself appear,
As doth the blushing discontented sun[22]
From out the fiery portal[23] of the east,
When he perceives the envious clouds are bent
To dim his glory, and to stain the track
Of his bright passage to the occident.[24]

YORK

Yet looks he like a king: behold, his eye,
As bright as is the eagle's,[25] lightens forth
Controlling majesty! Alack, alack, for woe,
That any harm should stain so fair a show![26]

KING RICHARD

We are amazed, and thus long have we stood
To watch the fearful bending of thy knee,[27]
Because we thought ourself thy lawful king.
And if we be, how dare thy joints forget
To pay their awful duty to our presence?[28]
If we be not, show us the hand of God,[29]
That hath dismissed us from our stewardship.
For well we know, no hand of blood and bone
Can gripe[30] the sacred handle of our sceptre

31 *torn their souls.* Richard speaks as if those who have turned to Bolingbroke have had to tear away their loyal hearts from supporting their king; they have injured their hearts in tearing them.

32 *barren, and bereft of friends* – "without power, and with all my friends taken from me".

33 *Is mustering . . . of pestilence.* Richard speaks as if, although he has no army, God is calling together (*mustering*) to fight for him (*on our behalf*) a number of plagues which will destroy (*strike*) even the unborn and unfathered (*unbegot*) children of every subject (*vassal*) who attacks the king.

34 *to open . . . face* – "to find out, by opening the blood-red (*purple*) will (*testament*) of murderous civil war, who will have the crown of England when the war is over; but before (*ere*) Bolingbroke can live in peace with the crown he hopes (*looks*) to inherit, many blood-stained heads (*crowns*) of Englishmen, whose mothers will sorrow at their deaths, shall make ugly (*ill become*) our country which is now lovely as a flower". Richard speaks as if Bolingbroke can inherit the crown of England only if war has written in its will that this is to be so. Bolingbroke can see what has been written by starting a civil war in England.

35 *Change the complexion . . . blood.* Richard speaks as if the peaceful face of England, pale as a young girl (*maid*), shall be changed to bright red (*scarlet*) with the blood of dying soldiers and with England's anger (*indignation*) that these men must die; blood will be seen, like dew, on the grass.

36 *The king of heaven . . . upon* – "God forbid that the king should be attacked with cruel (*uncivil*) weapons in civil war". (Northumberland knows that there can be civil war only if the king has an army, as Bolingbroke has.)

37 *thrice-noble* – "of noble rank on three counts", through his grandfather Edward III, through his father John of Gaunt, and in his own right.

38 *grandsire*, grandfather, Edward III.

39 *royalties . . . head* – "rights granted by the previous kings (*royalties*) to both your family and to his (*both your bloods*), and both these families descend from Edward III, like separate streams (*currents*) that have their beginning (*spring*) in one source (*head*)".

Unless he do profane, steal, or usurp.
And though you think that all, as you have done,
Have torn their souls[31] by turning them from us,
And we are barren, and bereft of friends;[32]
Yet know, my master, God omnipotent,
Is mustering in his clouds, on our behalf,
Armies of pestilence,[33] and they shall strike
Your children yet unborn, and unbegot,
That lift your vassal hands against my head,
And threat the glory of my precious crown.
Tell Bolingbroke – for yond methinks he stands –
That every stride he makes upon my land
Is dangerous treason: he is come to open
The purple testament of bleeding war;
But ere the crown he looks for live in peace,
Ten thousand bloody crowns of mothers' sons
Shall ill become the flower of England's face,[34]
Change the complexion of her maid-pale peace
To scarlet indignation, and bedew
Her pastures' grass with faithful English blood.[35]

NORTHUMBERLAND

The king of heaven forbid our lord the king
Should so with civil and uncivil arms
Be rushed upon![36] Thy thrice-noble[37] cousin,
Harry Bolingbroke, doth humbly kiss thy hand,
And by the honourable tomb he swears,
That stands upon your royal grandsire's[38] bones,
And by the royalties of both your bloods –
Currents that spring from one most gracious head –[39]
And by the buried hand of warlike Gaunt,
And by the worth and honour of himself,
Comprising all that may be sworn, or said,
His coming hither hath no further scope,
Than for his lineal royalties, and to beg
Enfranchisement immediate on his knees;

40 *no further scope . . . granted once* – "no further aim, than to ask for the rights granted by the king (*royalties*) to his family before and after him (*lineal*), and to beg for the right to return from banishment as a free citizen (*Enfranchisement*) at once (*immediate*); and as soon as ever (*once*) you, the king, have granted this (*Which*) . . .".

41 *commend* – "give over".

42 *barbéd steeds* – "horses (*steeds*) armed and equipped".

43 *To look so poorly* – "to seem so poor in courage".

44 *Till time lend friends* – "until after some time we find more supporters".

45 *dread* – "dreadful, to be feared".

46 *words of sooth* – "soothing words".

His barbed steeds[42] *to stables*

Which on thy royal party granted once,[40]
His glittering arms he will commend[41] to rust,
His barbéd steeds[42] to stables, and his heart
To faithful service of your majesty.
This swears he, as he is a prince, is just,
And as I am a gentleman, I credit him.

KING RICHARD

Northumberland, say thus the king returns:
His noble cousin is right welcome hither,
And all the number of his fair demands
Shall be accomplished without contradiction.
With all the gracious utterance thou hast,
Speak to his gentle hearing kind commends.

NORTHUMBERLAND *goes back to* BOLINGBROKE.
KING RICHARD *turns to* AUMERLE

We do debase ourselves, cousin, do we not,
To look so poorly,[43] and to speak so fair?
Shall we call back Northumberland, and send
Defiance to the traitor, and so die?

AUMERLE

No, good my lord; let 's fight with gentle words
Till time lend friends[44] and friends their helpful swords.

KING RICHARD

Oh, God, oh, God, that e'er this tongue of mine,
That laid the sentence of dread[45] banishment
On yon proud man, should take it off again
With words of sooth![46] Oh, that I were as great
As is my grief, or lesser than my name!
Or that I could forget what I have been,
Or not remember what I must be now!

47 *Swell'st thou* – "Do you swell with anger?"
48 *scope* – "space".
49 *scope* – "free play". If the king's heart swells with anger, he still cannot speak out; he can give his heart freedom simply to go on beating, but his enemies (*foes*) have freedom to attack him and his heart also.
50 *A'* – "In".
51 *set of beads* – "rosary".
52 *gay apparel . . . gown* – "brightly coloured dress for the long grey coat of an old pensioner". (*gown*, "long coat"; *almsman*, "an old beggar who said prayers for those who gave him alms, i.e. charity".
53 *of* – "made of".
54 *palmer's walking staff* – "stick which a pilgrim (*palmer*) carries".
55 *way of common trade* – "road where many people pass for buying and selling".
56 *buried once* – "when once I am buried".
57 *foul* – "stormy".
58 *and they, . . . land* – "and tears shall lay flat (*lodge*) the ripening (*summer*) corn and bring about a famine in this land which is rebelling (*revolting*) against its king".
59 *play the wantons* – "amuse ourselves in some frivolous way".
60 *make some pretty match* – "start some playful competition (*match*)".
61 *still* – "always".
62 *ill do well* – "sorrowful action be quite interesting?"

Swell'st thou,[47] proud heart? I 'll give thee scope[48] to beat,
Since foes have scope[49] to beat both thee and me.

AUMERLE

Northumberland comes back from Bolingbroke.

KING RICHARD

What must the king do now? Must he submit?
The king shall do it. Must he be deposed?
The king shall be contented. Must he lose
The name of king? A'[50] God's name, let it go.
I 'll give my jewels for a set of beads,[51]
My gorgeous palace for a hermitage,
My gay apparel for an almsman's gown,[52]
My figured goblets for a dish of[53] wood,
My sceptre for a palmer's walking staff,[54]
My subjects for a pair of carvéd saints,
And my large kingdom for a little grave,
A little, little grave, an obscure grave.
Or I 'll be buried in the king's high-way,
Some way of common trade,[55] where subjects' feet
May hourly trample on their sovereign's head;
For on my heart they tread now, whilst I live,
And buried once,[56] why not upon my head?
Aumerle, thou weep'st, my tender-hearted cousin!
We 'll make foul[57] weather with despiséd tears;
Our sighs, and they, shall lodge the summer corn,
And make a dearth in this revolting land.[58]
Or shall we play the wantons[59] with our woes,
And make some pretty match[60] with shedding tears?
As thus: to drop them still[61] upon one place,
Till they have fretted us a pair of graves,
Within the earth; and, therein laid, there lies
Two kinsmen, digged their graves with weeping eyes!
Would not this ill do well?[62] Well, well, I see

63 *but idly* – "only foolishly".

64 *Ay* – "yes".

65 *base court . . . attend* – "courtyard below (*base*) he is waiting . . .".

66 *glistering Phaëton . . . jades* – "glittering Phaëthon unable to control the wild and disobedient horses". In the old Greek legends, Phaëthon, son of the sun-god, at last persuaded his father to allow him for the whole of one day to drive the chariot of the sun across the sky. But he could not manage the horses, drove too near the earth, and was killed and thrown down. In the same way Richard suggests he himself, son of the Black Prince, could not control his disobedient subjects.

67 *base* – "ignoble".

68 *grace* – "honour".

69 *night-owls shriek . . . sing* – "instead of the sweet song of high-rising skylarks (sign of a young king's success) we hear the high loud cry (*shriek*) of the owl by night (a sign of evil to come)".

70 *fondly* – "foolishly".

I talk but idly,[63] and you laugh at me.
Most mighty prince, my Lord Northumberland,
What says King Bolingbroke? Will his majesty
Give Richard leave to live till Richard die?
You make a leg, and Bolingbroke says "Ay".[64]

NORTHUMBERLAND

My lord, in the base court he doth attend[65]
To speak with you, may it please you to come down.

KING RICHARD

Down, down I come, like glistering Phaëton,
Wanting the manage of unruly jades.[66]
In the base court? Base court, where kings grow base,[67]
To come at traitors' calls and do them grace.[68]
In the base court come down? Down, court, down, king,
For night-owls shriek where mounting larks should sing![69]

BOLINGBROKE

What says his majesty?

NORTHUMBERLAND

Sorrow and grief of heart
Makes him speak fondly[70] like a frantic man;
Yet he is come.

Enter KING RICHARD *and his* attendants *below.*

BOLINGBROKE

Stand all apart,
And show fair duty to his majesty. [*He kneels down*
My gracious lord, –

71 *Me rather had* – "I had rather".

72 *So far be mine . . . lord* – "My lord whom I fear greatly (*redoubtéd*), be a friend to me (*mine*) just as far . . .".

73 *Tears show . . . remedies* – "Men's tears show that they love me, but they show also that men lack (*want*) power to help me (*remedies*)".

74 *force will have us do* – "necessity requires us to do".

KING RICHARD

Fair cousin, you debase your princely knee
To make the base earth proud with kissing it.
Me rather had[71] my heart might feel your love
Than my unpleased eye see your courtesy.
Up, cousin, up! Your heart is up, I know,
Thus high at least, although your knee be low.

BOLINGBROKE

My gracious lord, I come but for mine own.

KING RICHARD

Your own is yours, and I am yours, and all.

BOLINGBROKE

So far be mine, my most redoubtéd lord,[72]
As my true service shall deserve your love.

KING RICHARD

Well you deserve. They well deserve to have
That know the strong'st and surest way to get.
Uncle, give me your hand: nay, dry your eyes;
Tears show their love, but want their remedies.[73]
Cousin, I am too young to be your father
Though you are old enough to be my heir.
What you will have, I 'll give, and willing too,
For do we must what force will have us do.[74]
Set on towards London, cousin, is it so?

BOLINGBROKE

Yea, my good lord.

KING RICHARD

Then I must not say no.

[Flourish. Exeunt

(III.iv) In the garden of the Duke of York's house at Langley, the queen can find no pleasure to lessen her sorrow. She and her ladies hide, so as to listen to the talk of the gardener and his men; the queen thinks that they will talk about the situation between the king and Bolingbroke. The gardener orders one of his men to tie up the branches of ripe apricots since the rich fruit is growing too heavy for the tree; another is to cut off the heads of the sprays which have grown too tall; he himself will root up the evil-smelling weeds. One of the servants asks why should they keep *this* garden in order while the garden of England is being spoilt for lack of care. The gardener answers that Richard has now lost his power; his favourites, the weeds of England's garden, have been plucked up by Bolingbroke, and it is likely that the king will be deposed. At this the queen comes forward and asks angrily how and when he heard this news. He answers that it is true; Richard is a prisoner of Bolingbroke and Bolingbroke has the support of all the English nobles. The queen decides to go to London to meet Richard again.

1 *sport . . . devise* – "amusement (*sport*) shall we plan (*devise*)".

2 *thought of care* – "thoughts of sorrow".

3 *rubs* – "obstacles" – e.g. an uneven piece of ground.

4 *my fortune . . . bias* – "my luck is against me"; (*bias*, weight fixed in the side of a bowl so that it will run in a certain curve).

5 *keep no measure . . . grief* – "keep up no pleasant rhythm (*measure*) in dancing, while my heart is over-full with sorrow" (*measure*, "moderate amount").

6 *being altogether wanting . . . remember* – "since joy is altogether lacking, it will remind . . .".

7 *being altogether had* – "since I have nothing but grief".

Scene IV. Langley. The Duke of York's garden.
Enter the QUEEN *and two* Ladies.

QUEEN

What sport shall we devise[1] here in this garden
To drive away the heavy thought of care?[2]

LADY

Madam, we 'll play at bowls.

QUEEN

'T will make me think the world is full of rubs,[3]
And that my fortune runs against the bias.[4]

LADY

Madam, we 'll dance.

QUEEN

My legs can keep no measure in delight,
When my poor heart no measure keeps in grief.[5]
Therefore no dancing, girl; some other sport.

LADY

Madam, we 'll tell tales

QUEEN

Of sorrow, or of joy?

LADY

Of either, madam.

QUEEN

Of neither, girl.
For if of joy, being altogether wanting,
It doth remember[6] me the more of sorrow;
Or if of grief, being altogether had,[7]

8 *want . . . complain* – "am short of, it is no use (*boots not*) complaining about".

9 *And I could sing . . . of thee.* The Queen means that if her sorrow were of the kind that could be made less by crying, she could cry for herself (and not need the tears of her lady) and, having eased her sorrow, could even sing also.

10 *My wretchedness . . . state* – "I would wager the weight of my misery (*wretchedness*) against anything of little value that they will talk about politics and the government."

11 *Against a change* – "before (*Against*) there is a change of ruler".

12 *woe . . . woe* – "disaster (*woe*) to the state is preceded by a feeling of sorrow (*woe*) in the individual".

13 *apricocks . . . weight* – "apricots, which like wild and disobedient (*unruly*) children, make their father (*sire*) bend (*Stoop*) under the heavy sorrow (*oppression*) of the weight of their extravagance (*prodigal weight*)". The apricots are likely to hurt the parent plant by growing too large; so children, growing too important and spending too much (as Richard has done), make their fathers poor.

14 *supportance* – "support".

15 *even* – "of equal height". (Richard allowed his favourites to grow too powerful.)

It adds more sorrow to my want of joy:
For what I have I need not to repeat;
And what I want it boots not to complain.[8]

LADY

Madam, I 'll sing.

QUEEN

'T is well that thou hast cause;
But thou shouldst please me better wouldst thou weep.

LADY

I could weep, madam, would it do you good.

QUEEN

And I could sing, would weeping do me good,
And never borrow any tear of thee.[9]

Enter a Gardener, *and two* Servants

But stay, here come the gardeners;
Let 's step into the shadow of these trees.
My wretchedness unto a row of pins,
They 'll talk of state;[10] for every one doth so,
Against a change;[11] woe is forerun with woe.[12]

[QUEEN *and* Ladies *retire*

GARDENER

[*To one of his men*] Go bind thou up yon dangling apricocks,
Which, like unruly children, make their sire
Stoop with oppression of their prodigal weight:[13]
Give some supportance[14] to the bending twigs.
[*To the other*] Go thou, and like an executioner,
Cut off the heads of too fast growing sprays,
That look too lofty in our commonwealth.
All must be even[15] in our government.

16 *noisome weeds . . . flowers* – "evil-smelling (*noisome*) weeds which, without being of any use (*profit*), draw up for themselves the richness (*fertility*) of the soil, taking it away from (*from*) flowers which are fresh and lovely (*wholesome*)". (The favourites of the king, as we have seen, would have taken away for themselves the rich lands of Bolingbroke.)

17 *compass of a pale* – "limits of a garden fence".

18 *form and due proportion . . . estate* – "order and keep everything in proper (*due*) size (*proportion*), giving a picture of just control (*firm estate*) as if our garden was a model of a whole country". While the gardeners do this, England itself is like a garden that is uncared for.

19 *knots disordered* – "her flower-beds (*knots*) in disorder".

20 *Hold thy peace!* – "Be silent!"

21 *suffered this disordered spring . . . leaf* – "allowed England's garden in the spring to be in such disorder has now himself come to autumn".

22 *The weeds . . . root and all.* Richard's favourites were like weeds and his far-extending power seemed like broad-spreading leaves to protect them; they appeared to support him (*hold him up*) but actually wasted his treasure (*eating him*); now Bolingbroke has completely destroyed them.

23 *That he had not . . . itself* – "that Richard did not tidy (*trimmed*) and put in order (*dressed*) his government of England as we do this garden, at the proper season (*time of year*) cutting the bark of our fruit trees to stop (*lest*) the garden (*it*) spoiling itself (*confounded itself*) through the trees having too much blossom (*too much riches*) when they are too full (*over-proud*) of sap and desire to grow (*blood*)". (By cutting off newly-growing shoots and some of the blossom, better fruit is obtained.)

You thus employed, I will go root away
The noisome weeds, which without profit suck
The soil's fertility from wholesome flowers.[16]

SERVANT

Why should we, in the compass of a pale,[17]
Keep law and form and due proportion,
Showing, as in a model, our firm estate,[18]
When our sea-walléd garden, the whole land,
Is full of weeds, her fairest flowers choked up,
Her fruit-trees all unpruned, her hedges ruined,
Her knots disordered,[19] and her wholesome herbs
Swarming with caterpillars.

GARDENER

Hold thy peace![20]
He that hath suffered this disordered spring,
Hath now himself met with the fall of leaf.[21]
The weeds that his broad-spreading leaves did shelter,
That seemed, in eating him, to hold him up,
Are plucked up, root and all,[22] by Bolingbroke.
I mean the Earl of Wiltshire, Bushy, Green.

SERVANT

What, are they dead?

GARDENER

They are; and Bolingbroke
Hath seized the wasteful king. Oh, what pity is it,
That he had not so trimmed and dressed his land
As we this garden, at time of year,
Do wound the bark, the skin of our fruit-trees,
Lest, being over-proud with sap and blood,
With too much riches it confound itself![23]

24 *Had he done so . . . duty.* If Richard had checked his powerful and ambitious favourites (*great and growing men*) they might have served him loyally and lived to be useful (*bear . . . fruits*) to the king and the state.

25 *that bearing boughs* – "so that boughs which bear good fruit".

26 *himself had borne* – "he himself would have gone on wearing . . .".

27 *Depressed . . . will be* – "He has already lost much of his power and it is likely (*doubt*) that he will be put off the throne".

28 *pressed to death.* Any person charged with an offence who refused to answer the charge was pressed to death by a heavy weight put on his chest. The queen feels as if she will die if she remains silent any longer.

29 *set to dress* – "appointed to keep in order . . .".

30 *suggested thee . . . man* – "persuaded you to speak about, as if it were true, a second downfall of man condemned by God (*curséd*)". In the Biblical story of the beginning of the world, Eve, persuaded by the serpent, disobeyed God and persuaded Adam also to do so. This was the first fall of mankind into sin. Proverbs speak of Adam as the first gardener so that the queen thinks of the Duke of York's gardener as a picture of the earlier Adam.

31 *ill tidings* – "very bad news".

32 *mighty hold* – "powerful grasp".

33 *weighed.* What will happen to Bolingbroke and to Richard is now in the balance; their power is weighed one against the other as if on the scales. Richard's side is light – it has only the king himself and some foolish things (*vanities*) in his character and actions; but Bolingbroke's side is heavy with all the English nobles (*peers*) supporting him, and with that difference (*odds*) between them he weighs down the king.

Had he done so to great and growing men,
They might have lived to bear, and he to taste
Their fruits of duty.[24] Superfluous branches
We lop away, that bearing boughs[25] may live.
Had he done so, himself had borne[26] the crown,
Which waste of idle hours hath quite thrown down.

SERVANT

What, think you then the king shall be deposed?

GARDENER

Depressed he is already, and deposed
'T is doubt he will be.[27] Letters came last night
To a dear friend of the good Duke of York's,
That tell black tidings.

QUEEN

Oh I am pressed to death[28] through want of speaking!
[*Coming forward*] Thou, old Adam's likeness, set to dress[29] this garden,
How dare thy harsh, rude tongue sound this unpleasing news?
What Eve, what serpent, hath suggested thee,
To make a second fall of curséd man?[30]
Why dost thou say King Richard is deposed?
Dar'st thou, thou little better thing than earth,
Divine his downfall? Say where, when, and how
Cam'st thou by this ill tidings?[31] Speak, thou wretch!

GARDENER

Pardon me, madam. Little joy have I
To breathe this news; yet what I say is true;
King Richard, he is in the mighty hold[32]
Of Bolingbroke; their fortunes both are weighed.[33]
In your lord's scale is nothing but himself,
And some few vanities that make him light;

34 *Post* – "Ride quickly".

35 *Nimble mischance . . . to me* – "Misfortune (*mischance*) which can move so swiftly (*Nimble*), with light quick steps, is it not to me that your message should be brought?" (*embassage*, "bringing of message".)

36 *grace* – "honour".

37 *so that thy state . . . curse* – if it would mean that things would be no worse for you, I would wish my knowledge of gardening and grafting (*skill*) taken away from me by your words".

38 *rue, sour herb of grace.* The name *rue* was thought to mean "repentance"; *herb of grace* (*grace* also meaning "repentance") was another name for this plant. The gardener is sorry that he added to the queen's grief.

39 *ruth* – "pity".

But in the balance of great Bolingbroke,
Besides himself, are all the English peers,
And with that odds he weighs King Richard down.
Post[34] you to London, and you 'll find it so;
I speak no more than every one doth know.

QUEEN

Nimble mischance, that art so light of foot,
Doth not thy embassage belong to me?[35]
And am I last that knows it? Oh, thou think'st
To serve me last, that I may longest keep
Thy sorrow in my breast. Come, ladies, go,
To meet at London London's king in woe.
What, was I born to this, that my sad look,
Should grace[36] the triumph of great Bolingbroke?
Gardener, for telling me these news of woe,
Pray God the plants thou graft'st may never grow.

[*Exeunt* QUEEN *and* Ladies

GARDENER

Poor queen, so that thy state might be no worse,
I would my skill were subject to thy curse![37]
Here did she fall a tear; here, in this place,
I 'll set a bank of rue, sour herb of grace.[38]
Rue, even for ruth,[39] here shortly shall be seen,
In the remembrance of a weeping queen.

[*Exeunt*

(IV.i) In Westminster Hall, Bolingbroke is about to declare himself king and he wants first to show that Richard was guilty of Gloucester's death and of injustice to himself. Bagot, former favourite of Richard, is called to give evidence. He tells how Aumerle plotted the death of Gloucester and wished also for the death of Bolingbroke. Aumerle denies that he ever said the words which Bagot quotes and challenges Bagot to fight. Fitzwater, Percy and another lord declare that Aumerle is lying; Surrey supports him. Fitzwater remembers that Norfolk once spoke of how Aumerle sent two of his men to execute the Duke of Gloucester at Calais. Bolingbroke promises that Norfolk shall be called back from banishment and receive his lands again; then they can return to this dispute; Carlisle tells them however that Norfolk has died in Italy. York, bringing word that Richard is willing to give up his throne to Bolingbroke, salutes him as King Henry the Fourth, and Bolingbroke, in God's name, takes his seat on the throne. There is one protest from the Bishop of Carlisle: he says that no subject can pass sentence on a king, that Richard should not be judged in his absence, and that civil war will follow from Bolingbroke's action. Northumberland promptly arrests him for high treason, but Bolingbroke accepts the second criticism made by Carlisle and asks for Richard to be brought into the Parliament Hall, so that all may see him surrender the crown. Richard gives the crown to Bolingbroke and Northumberland then asks him to read aloud a list confessing the crimes which he and his followers have committed. Richard answers that it is a crime also to depose a king; he cannot see to read this list because his eyes are full of tears. He asks for a mirror so that he may see what he looks like now that he is no longer a king, and throws the glass down to break on the ground. Bolingbroke makes known that he will be crowned king in a few days' time. Carlisle, Aumerle and the Abbot of Westminster begin to plot the death of Bolingbroke.

1 *as to.* The actors are to move forward as if in procession to the Parliament.

2 *wrought it with the king* – "persuaded the king to give orders for it".

3 *performed . . . end* – "carried out the murderous (*bloody*) duty (*office*) of causing his untimely (*timeless*) death".

4 *delivered* – "given out, spoken".

5 *dead time* – "time which threatened death".

6 *of length . . . restful* – "of a good length, to reach from the peaceful . . .".

7 *withal* – "in addition".

8 *blest* – "fortunate".

ACT FOUR

Scene I. London. Westminster Hall.

Enter, as to[1] *the Parliament,* BOLINGBROKE, AUMERLE, NORTHUMBERLAND, PERCY, FITZWATER, SURREY, *the* BISHOP OF CARLISLE, *the* ABBOT OF WESTMINSTER *and another* Lord, Herald, Officers, *and* BAGOT.

BOLINGBROKE

Call forth Bagot!
Now, Bagot, freely speak thy mind,
What thou dost know of noble Gloucester's death?
Who wrought it with the king,[2] and who performed
The bloody office of his timeless end?[3]

BAGOT

Then set before my face the Lord Aumerle.

BOLINGBROKE

Cousin, stand forth, and look upon that man.

BAGOT

My Lord Aumerle, I know your daring tongue
Scorns to unsay what once it hath delivered.[4]
In that dead time,[5] when Gloucester's death was plotted,
I heard you say, "Is not my arm of length,
That reacheth from the restful[6] English court
As far as Calais, to mine uncle's head?"
Amongst much other talk, that very time,
I heard you say that you had rather refuse
The offer of an hundred thousand crowns,
Than Bolingbroke's return to England;
Adding withal,[7] how blest[8] this land would be,
In this your cousin's death.

9 *base man* – "man of low birth and evil character".

10 *my fair stars . . . chastisement* – "the fortune of my noble birth to fight with him as an equal and give him his punishment"; (it was thought that the stars under which a man was born influenced whatever happened to him).

11 *attainder of his slanderous lips* – "dishonourable accusation (*attainder*) of his untrue and harmful (*slanderous*) words".

12 *gage, the manual seal of death* – "pledge (*gage*), the glove from my hand as a seal stamped by the hand of death"; (*manual*, "of the hand").

13 *In thy heart blood, . . . sword* – "by killing you, although you are of far too low birth (*all too base*) to mark with your blood the finely-hardened metal of my noble sword"; (*temper*, "to make a metal hard").

14 *one.* Bolingbroke himself.

15 *thy valour . . . sympathy* – "your courage (*valour*) in making the challenge requires (*stands on*) an enemy of equal rank (*sympathy*) . . .".

16 *turn . . . point* – "on my sword's (*rapier's*) point, bring back (*turn*) to your heart, which makes this false denial (*Where it was forgéd*), the lie you speak". Your heart's blood shall pay for your lie. (*rapier*, "long thin sword".)

AUMERLE

Princes, and noble lords:
What answer shall I make to this base man?[9]
Shall I so much dishonour my fair stars,
On equal terms to give him chastisement?[10]
Either I must, or have mine honour soiled
With the attainder of his slanderous lips.[11]
There is my gage, the manual seal of death[12]
That marks thee out for hell. I say, thou liest,
And will maintain what thou hast said is false,
In thy heart blood, though being all too base
To stain the temper of my knightly sword.[13]

BOLINGBROKE

Bagot, forbear; thou shalt not take it up.

AUMERLE

Excepting one,[14] I would he were the best
In all this presence that hath moved me so.

FITZWATER

If that thy valour stand on sympathy,[15]
There is my gage, Aumerle, in gage to thine:
By that fair sun which shows me where thou stand'st,
I heard thee say, and vauntingly thou spak'st it,
That thou wert cause of noble Gloucester's death.
If thou deniest it twenty times, thou liest,
And I will turn thy falsehood to thy heart
Where it was forgéd, with my rapier's point.[16]

AUMERLE

Thou dar'st not, coward, live to see that day.

FITZWATER

Now, by my soul, I would it were this hour.

17 *appeal* – "charge, accusation".

18 *on thee . . . breathing* – "against you, or on your body, to the furthest (*extremest*) point of life" i.e. until one of us dies.

19 *I task . . . holloa'd* – "I charge (*task*) the earth to swallow me up, if I am lying, Aumerle, who have sworn to what is untrue (*forsworn*) and I drive you on (*spur*) to take my challenge with just (*full*) as many accusations that you are lying (*lies*) as may be cried out . . .".

20 *sun to sun* – "sunrise to sunrise, 24 hours".

21 *Engage it to the trial* – "Pick it up and make an agreement (*Engage*) to try out by fighting (*trial*) the truth of what I say".

22 *Who sets me else?* – "Who else calls me to fight?"

23 *throw at* – "take a chance against"; (*throw*, "to throw a dice in a game of chance").

24 *in presence* – "there in person".

Westminster Hall

AUMERLE

Fitzwater, thou art damned to hell for this!

PERCY

Aumerle, thou liest; his honour is as true
In this appeal,[17] as thou art all unjust!
And that thou art so, there I throw my gage
To prove it on thee to the extremest point
Of mortal breathing.[18] Seize it, if thou dar'st.

AUMERLE

And if I do not, may my hands rot off,
And never brandish more revengeful steel
Over the glittering helmet of my foe.

ANOTHER LORD

I task the earth to the like, forsworn Aumerle,
And spur thee on with full as many lies
As may be holloa'd[19] in thy treacherous ear
From sun to sun.[20] There is my honour's pawn!
Engage it to the trial[21] if thou darest.

AUMERLE

Who sets me else?[22] By heaven, I 'll throw at[23] all.
I have a thousand spirits in one breast,
To answer twenty thousand such as you.

SURREY

My Lord Fitzwater, I do remember well
The very time Aumerle and you did talk.

FITZWATER

'T is very true! You were in presence[24] then,
And you can witness with me this is true.

25 *That lie . . . quiet* – "Your falsehood (*lie*) shall rest (*lie*) with such weight on my sword that my sword shall take (*render*) revenge until both speaker (*lie-giver*) and his falsehood (*that lie*) rest in a grave as silent . . .".

26 *In proof whereof . . . pawn* – "And to prove this true, there is the pledge (*pawn*) of my honour as a knight".

27 *fondly* – "foolishly". Fitzwater speaks of himself as an over-eager (*forward*) horse which needs no driving forward (*spur*).

28 *bond of faith . . . correction* – "promise (*bond*) that I speak the truth, i.e. my glove, and, as it were, a rope (*bond*) to tie you up so that you cannot escape my firm punishment (*correction*)"; (*bond* probably has two meanings here, "promise" and "something which ties").

29 *world* – "kingdom, reign".

30 *appeal* – "charge".

31 *repealed, to try his honour* – "called back from banishment, as my promise that I will test (*try*) his truth by fighting against him".

SURREY

As false, by heaven, as heaven itself is true!

FITZWATER

Surrey, thou liest!

SURREY

Dishonourable boy!
That lie shall lie so heavy on my sword
That it shall render vengeance and revenge
Till thou, the lie-giver, and that lie, do lie
In earth as quiet[25] as thy father's skull;
In proof whereof, there is my honour's pawn![26]
Engage it to the trial, if thou dar'st!

FITZWATER

How fondly[27] dost thou spur a forward horse!
If I dare eat, or drink, or breathe, or live,
I dare meet Surrey in a wilderness,
And spit upon him, whilst I say he lies,
And lies, and lies. There is my bond of faith,
To tie thee to my strong correction.[28]
As I intend to thrive in this new world,[29]
Aumerle is guilty of my true appeal.[30]
Besides, I heard the banished Norfolk say
That thou, Aumerle, didst sent two of thy men
To execute the noble duke at Calais.

AUMERLE

Some honest Christian trust me with a gage
That Norfolk lies! Here do I throw down this,
If he may be repealed, to try his honour.[31]

32 *These differences . . . gage* – "These quarrels (*differences*) shall all remain unsettled (*rest*) and the pledges (*gage*) to fight shall wait . . .".

33 *signories* – "rights and possessions".

34 *enforce his trial* – "urge on (*enforce*) the test (*trial*) of his truthfulness".

35 *Streaming the ensign . . . pagans* – "letting fly in the wind (*Streaming*) the flag (*ensign*) marked with the cross of Christ in fighting against evil and dark-skinned (*black*) non-Christians (*pagans*)". Christians fought against "pagans" to win back the Holy City, Jerusalem.

36 *toiled with works of* – "worn out with".

37 *the bosom of good old Abraham.* It was believed that the souls of the blessed were carried to heaven to the arms of the prophet Abraham.

38 *appellants* – "who make these accusations".

BOLINGBROKE

These differences shall all rest under gage,[32]
Till Norfolk be repealed. Repealed he shall be,
And, though mine enemy, restored again
To all his lands and signories.[33] When he 's returned,
Against Aumerle we will enforce his trial.[34]

CARLISLE

That honourable day shall ne'er be seen.
Many a time hath banished Norfolk fought
For Jesu Christ in glorious Christian field,
Streaming the ensign of the Christian Cross,
Against black pagans,[35] Turks, and Saracens;
And toiled with works of[36] war, retired himself
To Italy, and there at Venice gave
His body to that pleasant country's earth,
And his pure soul unto his captain Christ,
Under whose colours he had fought so long.

BOLINGBROKE

Why, bishop, is Norfolk dead?

CARLISLE

As surely as I live, my lord.

BOLINGBROKE

Sweet peace conduct his sweet soul to the bosom
Of good old Abraham.[37] Lords appellants,[38]
Your differences shall all rest under gage,
Till we assign you to your days of trial.

Enter YORK *with* attendants

39 *plume-plucked* – "humbled", the tuft of feathers (*plume*) on a bird's head or soldier's helmet pulled out (*plucked*).

40 *descending now from him* – "as if you are a descendant, a son, of the ex-king Richard".

41 *Worst . . . truth.* Although Carlisle is lowest (*Worst*) in rank it is most fitting (*best beseeming*) that he should speak, since he is an officer of the church.

42 *true noblesse . . . wrong* – "true nobility (*noblesse*) would direct (*learn*) him not to do (*forebearance from*) so evil an injustice".

43 *but they are by* – "without their being present".

44 *elect* – "chosen".

45 *planted* – "like a tree which has been planted and taken root".

46 *forfend it . . . a deed* – "God forbid (*forfend*) that in a Christian land (*climate*) those whose souls have been purified from guilt (*refined*) by Christ should do so evil (*heinous*), bad and wicked (*obscene*) an act".

YORK

Great Duke of Lancaster, I come to thee
From plume-plucked[39] Richard, who with willing soul
Adopts thee heir, and his high sceptre yields
To the possession of thy royal hand.
Ascend his throne, descending now from him,[40]
And long live Henry, of that name the Fourth.

BOLINGBROKE

In God's name, I 'll ascend the regal throne.

CARLISLE

Marry, God forbid!
Worst in this royal presence may I speak,
Yet best beseeming me to speak the truth.[41]
Would God that any in this noble presence
Were enough noble to be upright judge
Of noble Richard! Then true noblesse would
Learn him forbearance from so foul a wrong.[42]
What subject can give sentence on his king?
And who sits here that is not Richard's subject?
Thieves are not judged but they are by[43] to hear,
Although apparent guilt be seen in them:
And shall the figure of God's majesty,
His captain, steward, deputy elect,[44]
Anointed, crownéd, planted[45] many years,
Be judged by subject and inferior breath,
And he himself not present? Oh, forfend it, God,
That in a Christian climate, souls refined
Should show so heinous, black, obscene a deed![46]
I speak to subjects, and a subject speaks,
Stirred up by God, thus boldly for his king.
My Lord of Hereford here, whom you call king,
Is a foul traitor to proud Hereford's king.

47 *future ages . . . confound* – "men of future time (*ages*) shall suffer (*groan*) because of this evil deed. Peace shall be found among cruel Turks and unbelievers (*infidels*) rather than in England, the home (*seat*) of peace, and civil war, full of noise and excitement (*tumultuous*) shall destroy (*confound*) relative (*kin*) at the hand of relative and one member of a family (*kind*) at the hands of another".

48 *Golgotha . . . skulls.* Golgotha, the place outside Jerusalem where Christ was crucified; the name itself means "skull". So England shall become a place of cruelty and death.

49 *you raise . . . prove* – "you nobles support (*raise*) one branch of the royal family (*house*) against another, it will turn out (*prove*) to be a quarrel (*division*) most full of sorrow (*woefullest*) . . .".

50 *Lest child . . . Woe!* – "for fear that (*Lest*) future generations cry out against you in reproach".

51 *the commons' suit* – "what the House of Commons has asked" i.e. that Richard give up the throne and the reasons for his deposition be made known.

52 *in common view* – "in sight of all".

53 *be his conduct* – "bring him".

54 *beholding* – "beholden, indebted".

55 *little looked for at* – "have expected little from . . .".

And if you crown him, let me prophesy,
The blood of English shall manure the ground,
And future ages groan for this foul act.
Peace shall go sleep with Turks and infidels,
And, in this seat of peace, tumultuous wars
Shall kin with kin and kind with kind confound.[47]
Disorder, horror, fear, and mutiny
Shall here inhabit, and this land be called
The field of Golgotha and dead men's skulls![48]
Oh, if you raise this house against this house,
It will the woefullest division prove[49]
That ever fell upon this curséd earth.
Prevent, resist it, let it not be so,
Lest child, child's children cry against you "Woe!"[50]

NORTHUMBERLAND

Well have you argued, sir; and, for your pains,
Of capital treason we arrest you here.
My Lord of Westminster, be it your charge,
To keep him safely till his day of trial.
May it please you, lords, to grant the commons' suit?[51]

BOLINGBROKE

Fetch hither Richard, that in common view[52]
He may surrender; so we shall proceed
Without suspicion.

YORK

I will be his conduct.[53] [*Exit*

BOLINGBROKE

Lords, you that here are under our arrest,
Procure your sureties for your days of answer.
Little are we beholding[54] to your love,
And little looked for at[55] your helping hands.

Re-enter YORK, *with* RICHARD, *and* Officers *bearing the regalia*

56 *Wherewith* – "with which".
57 *favours* – "appearances, features".
58 *sometime cry "All hail!"* – "at some earlier time salute me with wishes of all good fortune".
59 *Am I both priest and clerk?* – "Am I to say the first line of the service and the second also?" In church the clerk led the people to answer the priest and say "Amen".
60 *owes* – "has".
61 *ever dancing* – "always moving up or down".

RICHARD

Alack, why am I sent for to a king,
Before I have shook off the regal thoughts
Wherewith[56] I reigned? I hardly yet have learned
To insinuate, flatter, bow, and bend my limbs.
Give sorrow leave awhile to tutor me
To this submission. Yet I well remember
The favours[57] of these men; were they not mine?
Did they not sometime cry "All hail!"[58] to me?
So Judas did to Christ: but he, in twelve,
Found truth in all but one; I, in twelve thousand, none.
God save the king! Will no man say "Amen"?
Am I both priest and clerk?[59] Well then, "Amen.
God save the king!" although I be not he:
And yet "Amen", if Heaven do think him me. . . .
To do what service am I sent for hither?

YORK

To do that office of thine own good will,
Which tired majesty did make thee offer:
The resignation of thy state and crown
To Henry Bolingbroke.

RICHARD

Give me the crown. Here, cousin, seize the crown;
Here, cousin;
On this side my hand and on that side thine.
Now is this golden crown like a deep well,
That owes[60] two buckets, filling one another,
The emptier ever dancing[61] in the air,
The other down, unseen, and full of water;
That bucket down and full of tears am I,
Drinking my griefs, whilst you mount up on high.

BOLINGBROKE

I thought you had been willing to resign.

62 *cares* – "responsibilities, sorrows".

63 *Your cares . . . yet still* – "As you are raised up (*set up*) your responsibilities (*cares*) increase, but that does not pull (*pluck*) down, or lessen, my sorrow. My sorrow (*care*) is caused by loss of responsibility (*care*), a result of the way I looked after things in the past (*by old care done*); your sorrow is to have gained responsibility, by lately (*new*) giving great attention (*care*) to matters of state. Although I give away my responsibilities, I have my sorrows still. They go with (*tend*) the crown, but still . . .".

64 *Ay, no . . . myself.* Richard says yes, no (interchanging like the buckets of the well). He cannot say "Yes" (*no "Ay"*) because he must be a thing which means no (*nothing*); he cannot say any "No" (*no "No"*) because he *does* agree to resign. Now, notice carefully, he says, (*mark me*), how I will take off my kingly state and ruin myself (*undo* means both "to undress" and "to ruin").

65 *kingly sway* – "royal power".

66 *my balm* – "the holy oil put on my head when I was crowned king".

67 *release . . . oaths* – "set men free from all sworn promises that they would do their duty as my subjects".

RICHARD

My crown I am, but still my griefs are mine:
You may my glories and my state depose,
But not my griefs; still am I king of those.

BOLINGBROKE

Part of your cares[62] you give me with your crown.

RICHARD

Your cares set up do not pluck my cares down.
My care is loss of care, by old care done;
Your care is gain of care, by new care won:
The cares I give, I have, though given away;
They tend the crown, yet still[63] with me they stay.

BOLINGBROKE

Are you contented to resign the crown?

RICHARD

Ay, no: no, "Ay", for I must nothing be:
Therefore no "No," for I resign to thee.
Now, mark me, how I will undo myself.[64]
I give this heavy weight from off my head,
And this unwieldy sceptre from my hand,
The pride of kingly sway[65] from out my heart.
With mine own tears I wash away my balm,[66]
With mine own hands I give away my crown,
With mine own tongue deny my sacred state,
With mine own breath release all duteous oaths;[67]
All pomp and majesty I do forswear:
My manors, rents, revenues I forgo;
My acts, decrees, and statutes I deny;
God pardon all oaths that are broke to me!
God keep all vows unbroke are made to thee!

68 *Make me . . . achieved.* Richard asks that, when all his office of king has been given up, he may feel no sorrow, and that Bolingbroke, who has obtained (*achieved*) everything, may enjoy all he has.

69 *an earthy pit* – "a grave".

70 *by confessing . . . deposed* – "through your confessing your crimes against the state, men can judge (*deem*) your deposition deserved (*worthily*)".

71 *ravel out My weaved-up follies* – "untwist (*ravel out*) the threads of my foolishness which form the fabric of my reign"; (*weave*, "to form threads into cloth or fabric").

72 *upon record* – "written down in a list".

73 *To read a lecture of them* – "to read out what had been got ready to be read aloud (*lecture*) about them".

74 *wouldst* – "were to read such a list".

75 *heinous article* – "very bad section".

76 *cracking the strong warrant* – "breaking the firm promise".

77 *that my wretchedness . . . myself* – "in my misery (*wretchedness*) I make myself angry and excited (*bait*)".

78 *Pilate.* When Pilate, Governor of Jerusalem, gave Christ to be crucified, he first washed his hands with public ceremony to free himself from the guilt of Christ's death. Those who show pity for Richard now are none the less guilty of his great misfortune (*sour cross*).

79 *dispatch* – "act quickly".

Make me, that nothing have, with nothing grieved,
And thou with all pleased, that hast all achieved.[68]
Long mayst thou live, in Richard's seat to sit,
And soon lie Richard in an earthy pit.[69]
God save King Henry, un-kinged Richard says,
And send him many years of sunshine days.
What more remains?

NORTHUMBERLAND

No more: but that you read
These accusations, and these grievous crimes,
Committed by your person, and your followers,
Against the state, and profit of this land;
That, by confessing them, the souls of men
May deem that you are worthily deposed.[70]

RICHARD

Must I do so? And must I ravel out
My weaved-up follies?[71] Gentle Northumberland,
If thy offences were upon record,[72]
Would it not shame thee, in so fair a troop,
To read a lecture of them?[73] If thou wouldst,[74]
There shouldst thou find one heinous article,[75]
Containing the deposing of a king
And cracking the strong warrant[76] of an oath,
Marked with a blot, damned in the book of heaven.
Nay, all of you that stand and look upon me,
Whilst that my wretchedness doth bait myself,[77]
Though some of you, with Pilate,[78] wash your hands,
Showing an outward pity, yet you Pilates
Have here delivered me to my sour cross,
And water cannot wash away your sin.

NORTHUMBERLAND

My lord, dispatch;[79] read o'er these articles.

80 *sort* – "large group".

81 *undeck the pompous body of* – "take away the ornaments of splendour from . . .".

82 *state, a peasant* – "made stateliness like a poor country labourer".

83 *haught* – "haughty, proud".

84 *not that name . . . usurped* – "even the name that was given me when I was baptised at the font has been taken from me (*usurped*)".

85 *winters.* The years he has lived seem to contain only winter.

86 *a mockery king of snow.* A figure of a king made, in mockery, out of snow, which would melt, as if in tears, before the increasing power, the rising sun, of Bolingbroke.

87 *my word be sterling yet* – "my word of command is still to call forth obedience (as money which is *sterling*, or true, will buy what is required)".

88 *Since it is bankrupt . . . majesty* – "now that it is no longer the face of one who can speak as a king"; (*bankrupt*, a man who cannot pay his debts and is not allowed to buy goods on credit).

RICHARD

Mine eyes are full of tears; I cannot see;
And yet salt water blinds them not so much
But they can see a sort[80] of traitors here.
Nay, if I turn mine eyes upon myself,
I find myself a traitor with the rest.
For I have given here my soul's consent
To undeck the pompous body of[81] a king,
Made glory base, and sovereignty a slave,
Proud majesty a subject, state, a peasant.[82]

NORTHUMBERLAND

My lord, –

RICHARD

No lord of thine, thou haught[83] insulting man,
No, nor no man's lord. I have no name, no title,
No, not that name was given me at the font,
But 't is usurped![84] Alack, the heavy day,
That I have worn so many winters[85] out
And know not now what name to call myself!
Oh, that I were a mockery king of snow,[86]
Standing before the sun of Bolingbroke,
To melt myself away in water-drops!
Good king, great king, and yet not greatly good,
And if my word be sterling yet[87] in England,
Let it command a mirror hither straight,
That it may show me what a face I have,
Since it is bankrupt of his majesty.[88]

BOLINGBROKE

Go, some of you, and fetch a looking-glass.

[*Exit an* attendant

89 *the very book indeed*, his own face.

90 *Hath sorrow struck . . . beguile me.* Richard is surprised that his face does not look more sad. He believes that the mirror flatters and deceives (*beguile*) him as his followers did in the time of his good fortune.

91 *wink* – "blink their eyes, because they could not look at one so splendid and powerful".

92 *that faced . . . out-faced* – "that gave approval and support to (*faced*) so many foolish things done by his friends, and was finally out-dared . . ." (*faced*, "lined", as, for instance, a coat is lined with some other material, and so "supported").

93 *A brittle . . . face* – "The splendour that shows in this face in the mirror is soon broken; so too the glass and the face seen in it will break quickly".

94 *shivers* – "thin broken pieces".

95 *Mark . . . face* – "Notice (*Mark*), silent king, the hidden meaning (*moral*) of this jest (*sport*), how soon the face of a king can be destroyed by sorrow".

NORTHUMBERLAND

Read o'er this paper, while the glass doth come.

RICHARD

Fiend, thou torment'st me ere I come to hell.

BOLINGBROKE

Urge it no more, my Lord Northumberland.

NORTHUMBERLAND

The Commons will not then be satisfied.

RICHARD

They shall be satisfied; I 'll read enough,
When I do see the very book indeed,[89]
Where all my sins are writ, and that 's myself.
Re-enter attendant *with glass*
Give me the glass, and therein will I read.
No deeper wrinkles yet? Hath sorrow struck
So many blows upon this face of mine,
And made no deeper wounds? Oh, flattering glass,
Like to my followers in prosperity,
Thou dost beguile me![90] Was this face the face
That every day, under his household roof,
Did keep ten thousand men? Was this the face
That, like the sun, did make beholders wink?[91]
Was this the face that faced so many follies
And was at last out-faced[92] by Bolingbroke?
A brittle glory shineth in this face;
As brittle as the glory is the face;[93]
[*Dashes the glass to the ground*
For there it is, cracked in a hundred shivers.[94]
Mark, silent king, the moral of this sport,
How soon my sorrow hath destroyed my face.[95]

96 *The shadow . . . face* – "It was an unreal face that your sorrow destroyed and your sorrow too is not quite real".

97 *lies all within . . . shadows to* – "is all inside; and this way (*manner*) of complaining (*laments*) on the outside (*external*) is only a shadow compared to . . .".

98 *There lies the substance* – "The real weight (*substance*) of sorrow is in the heart".

99 *giv'st Me cause . . . cause* – "gives me reason to cry out, but shows (*teachest*) me the proper way to complain (*lament*) about the reason".

BOLINGBROKE

The shadow of your sorrow hath destroyed
The shadow of your face.[96]

RICHARD

Say that again.
The shadow of my sorrow? Ha, let 's see:
'T is very true, my grief lies all within;
And these external manner of laments,
Are merely shadows to[97] the unseen grief,
That swells with silence in the tortured soul.
There lies the substance:[98] and I thank thee, king,
For thy great bounty, that not only giv'st
Me cause to wail, but teachest me the way
How to lament the cause.[99] I 'll beg one boon,
And then be gone, and trouble you no more.
Shall I obtain it?

BOLINGBROKE

Name it, fair cousin.

RICHARD

"Fair cousin"? I am greater than a king;
For when I was a king, my flatterers
Were then but subjects; being now a subject,
I have a king here to my flatterer.
Being so great, I have no need to beg.

BOLINGBROKE

Yet ask.

RICHARD

And shall I have?

100 *so I were from your sights* – "so long as I were out of sight of you all".
101 *Tower*, fortress-palace of London, used as a prison for noblemen and kings.
102 "*Convey*"? The word means both "to take" and "to cheat".
103 *the children yet unborn . . . thorn* – "future generations shall suffer for what has been done today".
104 *pernicious blot* – "wicked stain" (of Bolingbroke's taking the crown).

convey him to the Tower[101]

BOLINGBROKE

You shall.

RICHARD

Then give me leave to go.

BOLINGBROKE

Whither?

RICHARD

Whither you will, so I were from your sights.[100]

BOLINGBROKE

Go, some of you, convey him to the Tower.[101]

RICHARD

Oh, good! "Convey"?[102] Conveyors are you all
That rise thus nimbly by a true king's fall.
[*Exeunt* RICHARD, *some* Lords *and* guards

BOLINGBROKE

On Wednesday next we solemnly set down
Our coronation: lords, prepare yourselves.
Exeunt all except BISHOP OF CARLISLE, ABBOT OF WESTMINSTER *and* AUMERLE

ABBOT

A woeful pageant have we here beheld.

CARLISLE

The woe 's to come; the children yet unborn
Shall feel this day as sharp to them as thorn.[103]

AUMERLE

You holy clergymen, is there no plot
To rid the realm of this pernicious blot?[104]

105 *Before I freely . . . devise* – "Before I say fully and openly (*freely*) what is in my mind about this, you must take the holy bread and wine (*sacrament*) as a promise that you will keep secret (*bury*) my purpose (*intents*) and also will carry out (*effect*) whatever later I may plan (*devise*)".

106 *brows* – "expressions" (*brow*, "forehead").

107 *lay* – "make".

ABBOT

My lord,
Before I freely speak my mind herein,
You shall not only take the sacrament
To bury mine intents, but also to effect
Whatever I shall happen to devise.[105]
I see your brows[106] are full of discontent,
Your hearts of sorrow, and your eyes of tears.
Come home with me to supper, and I 'll lay[107]
A plot shall show us all a merry day!

[*Exeunt*

(v.i) The Queen is waiting to see Richard pass by on his way to the Tower. He asks her to go home to France and enter a convent there; she is angry that he is ready to accept his fate. Northumberland brings an order from Bolingbroke that Richard is to go to Pomfret (in the north of England) instead of remaining in London at the Tower; the Queen is to leave for France at once. Richard warns Northumberland of an evil fate to come upon him. He does not believe that Northumberland and Bolingbroke will remain friends: Northumberland will want a larger reward and Bolingbroke will fear and hate him.

1 *Julius Caesar's . . . flint bosom.* It was an old belief that Julius Caesar (the famous Roman general who came to England in 55 B.C.) first built the Tower of London. The Queen wishes that the Tower had never been built (*ill-erected*, "built for an unlucky purpose"); it is built of flint, a very hard stone and in its hard heart (*bosom*) Richard is to be imprisoned.

2 *if this rebellious earth . . . resting* – "if the earth of England, which has rebelled against its true king, will allow the queen to wait quietly . . .".

3 *soft* – "wait for a moment".

4 *My fair rose wither.* Richard who had seemed to her lovely as a rose now looks old and tired. Their tears, like dew on a flower, might make him fresh and young again.

5 *the model . . . Richard.* Troy, one of the greatest cities of an earlier civilisation, is now in ruins. So Richard, who still has the shape (*model*) he had when he was king, has none of the power and splendour; he is like a map, an unreal paper plan of honour; his body is living but King Richard is dead.

6 *most beauteous inn . . . ale-house guest* – "Why should harsh-looking (*hard-favoured*) sorrow have its place or lodging in one who is like a most beautiful house (*inn*) where guests can stay, while pleasure in success (*triumph*) stays with Bolingbroke, as a person might stay in a common drinking-house (*ale-house*)?" She would expect the best guest to stay in the best inn.

7 *Join not with grief . . . sudden.* Richard speaks to his wife (*fair woman*) as if to a stranger, since now they must part for ever. Her grief added to his own might make him die of sorrow at once (*make my end too sudden*).

8 *I am sworn brother . . . death* – "Cruel need (*grim necessity*) and myself have made a solemn promise that we will act like brothers and fight side by side (*keep a league*) until death separate us". This promise takes the place of his marriage vow to his queen.

9 *Hie thee . . . down* – "Go quickly (*Hie thee*) to France, and find a place in the cloisters of some nunnery (*religious house*). We must in the future, by holy lives, apart from the world, win in heaven (*new world*) the crown which our unholy (*profane*) life here has lost".

ACT FIVE

Scene I. London. A street leading to the Tower.

Enter QUEEN *and* Ladies.

QUEEN

This way the king will come; this is the way
To Julius Caesar's ill-erected tower,
To whose flint bosom[1] my condemnéd lord
Is doomed a prisoner by proud Bolingbroke.
Here let us rest, if this rebellious earth
Have any resting[2] for her true king's queen.

Enter RICHARD *and* Guard.

But soft,[3] but see, or rather do not see,
My fair rose wither;[4] yet look up; behold,
That you in pity may dissolve to dew,
And wash him fresh again with true-love tears.
Ah thou, the model where old Troy did stand,
Thou map of honour, thou King Richard's tomb,
And not King Richard:[5] thou most beauteous inn,
Why should hard-favoured grief be lodged in thee,
When triumph is become an ale-house guest?[6]

RICHARD

Join not with grief, fair woman, do not so,
To make my end too sudden;[7] learn, good soul,
To think our former state a happy dream,
From which awaked, the truth of what we are,
Shows us but this. I am sworn brother, sweet,
To grim necessity; and he and I
Will keep a league till death.[8] Hie thee to France,
And cloister thee in some religious house:
Our holy lives must win a new world's crown,
Which our profane hours here have stricken down.[9]

10 *Deposed thine intellect* – "taken away your mind as well as your throne".

11 *The lion dying . . . beasts* – "A lion does not die quietly, but pushes out (*thrusteth forth*) its paw and if it can wound nothing else, at least it tears the ground in its anger (*rage*) at being overcome. Then will you, who are a lion and ruler of the animal kingdom, behave like a school-boy (*pupil-like*), accept your punishment (*correction*) without anger (*mildly*), kiss the stick (*rod*) with which you are to be punished (as schoolboys then were made to do) and with ignoble (*base*) humbleness (*humility*) meet the anger (*rage*) of Bolingbroke with flattery, like a dog wanting to be stroked (*fawn on*)?"

12 *if aught but beasts . . . queen* – "if my subjects had been anything (*aught*) except (*but*) cruel and stupid animals, I should still have been ruling happily over men. My gentle (*Good*) queen of former times (*sometime*) . . .".

13 *thy last living leave* – "your last farewell (*leave*) while you live in this world (*living*)".

14 *ages, long ago betid* – "times, which happened (*betid*) long ago".

15 *to quit their griefs* – "to repay them (*quit*) for the sad tales they have told you (*their griefs*)".

16 *For why . . . coal-black* – "And the reason is that even the burning pieces of wood on the fire (*brands*), which have no feeling (*senseless*), will sympathise with the sad tone (*heavy accent*) of your moving words, and in pity (*compassion*) will put out the fire as if with tears; some of the wood will turn to grey ashes (which people sometimes put on their heads as a sign of mourning), some will be black as charcoal in sorrow . . ." (*charcoal*, "wood blackened in the fire").

17 *there is order ta'en* – "directions have been given".

QUEEN

What, is my Richard both in shape and mind
Transformed and weakened? Hath Bolingbroke
Deposed thine intellect?[10] Hath he been in thy heart?
The lion dying thrusteth forth his paw,
And wounds the earth, if nothing else, with rage
To be o'erpowered; and wilt thou, pupil-like,
Take thy correction mildly, kiss the rod,
And fawn on rage with base humility,
Which art a lion, and a king of beasts?[11]

RICHARD

A king of beasts indeed; if aught but beasts,
I had been still a happy king of men.
Good sometime queen,[12] prepare thee hence for France:
Think I am dead, and that even here thou tak'st
As from my death-bed, thy last living leave.[13]
In winter's tedious nights sit by the fire
With good old folks, and let them tell thee tales
Of woeful ages, long ago betid;[14]
And ere thou bid good night, to quit their griefs,[15]
Tell thou the lamentable tale of me
And send the hearers weeping to their beds;
For why, the senseless brands will sympathise
The heavy accent of thy moving tongue,
And in compassion weep the fire out;
And some will mourn in ashes, some coal-black,[16]
For the deposing of a rightful king.

Enter NORTHUMBERLAND *and* others

NORTHUMBERLAND

My lord, the mind of Bolingbroke is changed.
You must to Pomfret, not unto the Tower.
And Madam, there is order ta'en[17] for you:
With all swift speed, you must away to France.

18 *wherewithal* – "with which".

19 *The time . . . corruption* – "it will not be long before (*ere*) evil sin in you, like a boil coming to a head (*gathering head*), shall burst (*break*) and let out its poisonous matter (*corruption*)".

20 *helping him to all* – "when you have helped him to get everything".

21 *plant unrightful kings* – "set firmly in place a king who has no right to the throne".

22 *ne'er so little . . . way* – "pushed on (*urged*) only a little (*ne'er so little*) in a different direction".

23 *The love . . . danger* – "The friendship (*love*) which two wicked men have for each other turns (*converts*) to fear and fear changes to hatred; hatred brings either one man, or both of them, to deserved (*worthy*) danger . . .".

24 *on my head* – "my own responsibility".

25 *unkiss the oath* – "in kissing you, undo the marriage promise . . .".

26 *pines the clime* – "makes the country (*clime*) suffer cold".

27 *set forth in pomp . . . day* – "sent on her way (*set forth*) in splendour (*pomp*), she came to England (*hither*) beautifully dressed (*addornéd*) and welcome as spring (*like sweet May*), but now she is sent back like an unwanted winter feast day (*Hallowmas*, "All Saints' Day", November 1) or like the shortest day of the year (December 21)".

RICHARD

Northumberland, thou ladder wherewithal[18]
The mounting Bolingbroke ascends my throne,
The time shall not be many hours of age,
More than it is, ere foul sin, gathering head,
Shall break into corruption;[19] thou shalt think,
Though he divide the realm, and give thee half,
It is too little, helping him to all;[20]
And he shall think that thou, which knowest the way
To plant unrightful kings,[21] wilt know again,
Being ne'er so little urged another way,[22]
To pluck him headlong from the usurpéd throne.
The love of wicked men converts to fear;
That fear, to hate; and hate turns one, or both,
To worthy danger,[23] and deservéd death.

NORTHUMBERLAND

My guilt be on my head,[24] and there an end!
Take leave, and part, for you must part forthwith.

RICHARD

Doubly divorced? Bad men, you violate
A twofold marriage; 'twixt my crown and me,
And then betwixt me and my married wife.
Let me unkiss the oath[25] 'twixt thee and me;
And yet not so, for with a kiss 't was made.
Part us, Northumberland! I towards the north,
Where shivering cold and sickness pines the clime;[26]
My wife to France: from whence, set forth in pomp,
She came adornéd hither like sweet May,
Sent back like Hallowmas, or short'st of day.[27]

QUEEN

And must we be divided? Must we part?

28 *policy,* "wisdom in looking after the state".

29 *be ne'er the near* – "never be the nearer (*near*)". Since we cannot be together it is better to be far apart.

30 *count thy way with sighs* – "sigh at every step".

31 *So longest way.* As she has the longest distance to go, so she will express her greater sorrow.

32 *piece the way out* – "make my journey seem longer".

33 *In wooing sorrow . . . grief* – "We shall each be married for a long time to sorrow, so let us not say very much in persuading (*wooing*) sorrow to be married to us". (At our wedding we kissed each other; with this kiss of parting we shall be wedded to grief. Let us kiss therefore and be silent.)

34 *Give me mine own . . . thy heart* – "If (with the first parting kiss) you have taken my heart, kiss me again to give it back. It would not be right (*no good part*) for me to undertake to keep your heart and let it die of sorrow with me".

RICHARD

Ay, hand from hand, my love, and heart from heart.

QUEEN

Banish us both and send the king with me.

NORTHUMBERLAND

That were some love but little policy.[28]

QUEEN

Then whither he goes, thither let me go.

RICHARD

So two, together weeping, make one woe.
Weep thou for me in France; I for thee here.
Better far off than near; be ne'er the near![29]
Go count thy way with sighs;[30] I mine with groans.

QUEEN

So longest way[31] shall have the longest moans.

RICHARD

Twice for one step I'll groan, the way being short,
And piece the way out[32] with a heavy heart.
Come, come! In wooing sorrow, let 's be brief,
Since, wedding it, there is such length in grief.[33]
One kiss shall stop our mouths, and dumbly part;
Thus give I mine, and thus take I thy heart.

QUEEN

Give me mine own again; 't were no good part
To take on me to keep and kill thy heart.[34]
So, now I have mine own again, be gone,
That I may strive to kill it with a groan.

35 *We make woe . . . delay* – "We turn sorrow into a frivolous game (*make woe wanton*) by this foolish (*fond*) delay".

(v.ii) York is describing to his wife how Bolingbroke and Richard came riding into London (from Flint Castle, before Richard's deposition). The crowds welcomed Bolingbroke but no one cried out "God save Richard!" Now, says York, Bolingbroke is king and they have sworn to be loyal to him. Their son, Aumerle, now to be called Rutland since he has lost his dukedom because of his support of Richard, comes in; he seems excited and anxious. York notices a seal hanging down from inside his coat and demands to see what is written on the paper. He snatches it out and reads it and sets off to the new king to report a plot against him. The Duchess of York tells her son to ride faster and ask for a pardon from the king; she herself will follow.

1 *misgoverned* – "ill-behaved".

2 *a hot and fiery steed . . . know* – "an eager and fiery-tempered horse, which seemed to know and sympathise with its ambitious (*aspiring*) rider".

3 *darted . . . visage* – "quickly fixed their eager (*desiring*) eyes on his face (*visage*)".

4 *With painted imagery*. You would have thought that the walls were painted cloths, i.e. hangings for a room painted or worked with figures and mottos of welcome.

RICHARD

We make woe wanton with this fond delay:[35]
Once more, adieu! The rest, let sorrow say!

[*Exeunt*

Scene II. The DUKE OF YORK'S *palace.*

Enter YORK *and his* DUCHESS.

DUCHESS

My lord, you told me you would tell the rest,
When weeping made you break the story off,
Of our two cousins coming into London.

YORK

Where did I leave?

DUCHESS

At that sad stop, my lord,
Where rude misgoverned[1] hands, from windows' tops,
Threw dust and rubbish on King Richard's head.

YORK

Then, as I said, the Duke, great Bolingbroke,
Mounted upon a hot and fiery steed,
Which his aspiring rider seemed to know,[2]
With slow but stately pace kept on his course,
Whilst all tongues cried "God save thee Bolingbroke!"
You would have thought the very windows spake,
So many greedy looks of young and old,
Through casements darted their desiring eyes
Upon his visage;[3] and that all the walls
With painted imagery[4] had said at once,
"Jesu preserve thee; welcome, Bolingbroke!"
Whilst he, from one side to the other turning,

5 *well-graced* – "much liked".
6 *idly* – "without paying much attention".
7 *His face still combating . . . patience.* Soldiers in King Richard's time wore *badges* to show on which side they were fighting. On Richard's face tears of grief and smiles of patience went on (*still*) fighting against each other (*combating*).
8 *steeled . . . barbarism itself* – "turned men's hearts into hard steel, they would necessarily (*perforce*) have melted into sympathy, and even the most savage unfeeling men (*barbarism itself*) . . .".
9 *heaven hath a hand . . . contents* – "it is God whose hand directs these happenings (*events*) and his holy command (*high will*) we accept in peace (*calm*) and gladness (*contents*)".
10 *aye allow* – "ever submit to".
11 *that* – "his dukedom and title".

Bare-headed, lower than his proud steed's neck,
Bespake them thus: "I thank you, countrymen!"
And thus still doing, thus he passed along.

DUCHESS

Alack, poor Richard! Where rode he the while?

YORK

As in a theatre, the eyes of men,
After a well-graced[5] actor leaves the stage,
Are idly[6] bent on him that enters next,
Thinking his prattle to be tedious;
Even so, or with much more contempt, men's eyes
Did scowl on gentle Richard; no man cried "God save him!"
No joyful tongue gave him his welcome home,
But dust was thrown upon his sacred head,
Which with such gentle sorrow he shook off,
His face still combating with tears and smiles –
The badges of his grief and patience –[7]
That had not God, for some strong purpose, steeled
The hearts of men, they must perforce have melted,
And barbarism itself[8] have pitied him.
But heaven hath a hand in these events,
To whose high will we bound our calm contents.[9]
To Bolingbroke are we sworn subjects now,
Whose state and honour I for aye allow.[10]

Enter AUMERLE

DUCHESS

Here comes my son Aumerle.

YORK

Aumerle that was,
But that[11] is lost for being Richard's friend,
And, madam, you must call him Rutland now;

12 *I am . . . fealty* – "I have in Parliament promised to be responsible (*pledge*) for his true service and lasting loyalty (*fealty*) . . .".

13 *the violets now . . . spring* – "the welcome little flowers scattered (*strew*) on the green grass of this fresh spring" i.e. the new favourites who crowd around the new king to win his good-will.

14 *as lief be none as one* – "as soon (*lief*) not be there".

15 *bear you well . . . prime* – "behave yourself well in this new reign, for fear (*Lest*) you are cut down (*cropped*) before you are fully grown into flower (*come to prime*)".

16 *Hold those . . . triumphs* – "Are those matches and tournaments to take place?" (*joust*, "combat in which two knights on horseback fought for a prize"; *triumph*, "tournament, competition in knightly sports".)

17 *that hangs without thy bosom* – "hanging outside from some paper you have stuffed into your coat".

Hold those jousts and triumphs[16]

I am in Parliament pledge for his truth,
And lasting fealty[12] to the new-made king.

DUCHESS

Welcome, my son! Who are the violets now
That strew the green lap of the new-come spring?[13]

AUMERLE

Madam, I know not, nor I greatly care not.
God knows I had as lief be none as one.[14]

YORK

Well, bear you well in this new spring of time
Lest you be cropped before you come to prime![15]
What news from Oxford? Hold those jousts and triumphs?[16]

AUMERLE

For aught I know, my lord, they do.

YORK

You will be there, I know.

AUMERLE

If God prevent not, I purpose so.

YORK

What seal is that that hangs without thy bosom?[17]
Yea, look'st thou pale? Let me see the writing!

AUMERLE

My lord, 't is nothing.

YORK

No matter then who see it;
I will be satisfied; let me see the writing.

18 *consequence* – "importance".

19 *bond . . . day* – "agreement that he has made for brightly coloured clothes (*gay apparel*), ready for (*'gainst*) the day of the tournament".

20 *Bound to himself.* If Aumerle had promised to pay a tailor, for instance, the tailor would have the agreement, not Aumerle. York is afraid that since Aumerle has a written agreement hidden away, others have made *him* an important promise.

AUMERLE

I do beseech your grace to pardon me;
It is a matter of small consequence,[18]
Which for some reasons I would not have seen.

YORK

Which for some reasons, sir, I mean to see:
I fear, I fear –

DUCHESS

What should you fear?
'T is nothing but some bond, that he is entered into
For gay apparel, 'gainst the triumph day.[19]

YORK

Bound to himself?[20] What doth he with a bond
That he is bound to? Wife, thou art a fool.
Boy, let me see the writing.

AUMERLE

I do beseech you, pardon me; I may not show it.

YORK

I will be satisfied: let me see it, I say!

[*Snatches it and reads it*

Treason, foul treason! Villain, traitor, slave!

DUCHESS

What is the matter, my lord?

YORK

[*shouts*] Hoa, who is within there? [*Enter a* Servant] Saddle my horse!
God, for his mercy! What treachery is here?

21 *my troth . . . villian* – "my loyalty, I will charge this evil man with treason".

22 *Peace* – "Be silent".

23 *him*, the servant.

DUCHESS

Why, what is 't, my lord?

YORK

Give me my boots, I say! Saddle my horse. [*Exit* Servant
Now by my honour, by my life, my troth,
I will appeach the villain![21]

DUCHESS

What is the matter?

YORK

Peace,[22] foolish woman!

DUCHESS

I will not peace. What is the matter, Aumerle?

AUMERLE

Good mother, be content; it is no more
Than my poor life must answer.

DUCHESS

Thy life answer?

YORK

Bring me my boots; I will unto the king.

Re-enter Servant *with boots*

DUCHESS

Strike him,[23] Aumerle. Poor boy, thou art amazed.
Hence, villain! Never more come in my sight.

YORK

Give me my boots, I say.

24 *trespass of thine own* – "crime of your own family".

25 *teeming date . . . with time* – "age for bearing children (*teeming date*) passed".

26 *ta'en the sacrament . . . hands* – "promised solemnly as they took the holy bread and wine, and each signed the others' papers".

27 *be none* – "not be one of them".

28 *what is that to him?* – "how does that make him guilty?"

29 *groaned for him*, in giving him birth.

DUCHESS

Why, York, what wilt thou do?
Wilt thou not hide the trespass of thine own?[24]
Have we more sons? Or are we like to have?
Is not my teeming date drunk up with time?[25]
And wilt thou pluck my fair son from mine age,
And rob me of a happy mother's name?
Is he not like thee? Is he not thine own?

YORK

Thou fond, mad woman:
Wilt thou conceal this dark conspiracy?
A dozen of them here have ta'en the sacrament,
And interchangeably set down their hands[26]
To kill the king at Oxford.

DUCHESS

He shall be none;[27]
We 'll keep him here: then what is that to him?[28]

YORK

Away fond woman! Were he twenty times my son,
I would appeach him.

DUCHESS

Hadst thou groaned for him[29]
As I have done, thou would'st be more pitiful!
But now I know thy mind; thou dost suspect
That I have been disloyal to thy bed,
And that he is a bastard, not thy son.
Sweet York, sweet husband, be not of that mind!
He is as like thee as a man may be,
Not like to me, or any of my kin,
And yet I love him.

30 *Spur post . . . before him to* – "Ride fast and arrive before he does to see . . .".

31 *doubt not but to* – "am sure that I can".

(v.iii) Bolingbroke, now King Henry the Fourth, asks for news of his eldest son whom he has not seen for over three months, a young man who prefers the taverns to the court. Bolingbroke hopes that he may later sober down into a good king. (In his next two history plays, *Henry IV*, Part I and Part II, Shakespeare shows Prince Hal as a rather wild young man, but honourable and courageous, to become in *Henry V* one of the greatest of England's kings.) Aumerle rushes in and asks to speak to the king alone. He kneels to ask for pardon and Bolingbroke promises to grant this if his offence has been planned only, but not committed. Aumerle, by Bolingbroke's permission, locks the door while he explains, but York arrives and insists on entering. York shows the paper he has taken from Aumerle and asks for death for his son. Now the Duchess of York is let in and kneels with her son to beg for his pardon. Aumerle is forgiven but Bolingbroke intends to capture the others who have plotted to kill him.

1 *unthrifty* – "good for nothing".

2 *If any . . . over us* – "If anything seems to threaten the safety of this kingdom . . .". Bolingbroke is afraid that Prince Hal, his eldest son, will not be serious enough to take the throne and rule well on his father's death.

3 *daily doth frequent* – "is to be found every day".

4 *unrestrainèd, loose* – "law-breaking, and of immoral (*loose*) life".

5 *watch* – "watchmen", the police-force of Shakespeare's time.

6 *passengers* – "travellers".

7 *Which he . . . a crew* – "and he, frivolous (*wanton*) young boy, too soft to fight in serious warfare (*effeminate*), thinks it the highest point of honour to be a member of such an immoral (*dissolute*) gang (*crew*)".

YORK

Make way, unruly woman!

[*Exit*

DUCHESS

After, Aumerle! Mount thee upon his horse,
Spur post, and get before him to[30] the king
And beg thy pardon, ere he do accuse thee.
I 'll not be long behind! Though I be old,
I doubt not but to[31] ride as fast as York,
And never will I rise up from the ground,
Till Bolingbroke have pardoned thee. Away, be gone!

[*Exeunt*

Scene III. A royal palace.

Enter BOLINGBROKE, PERCY, *and other* Lords.

BOLINGBROKE

Can no man tell me of my unthrifty[1] son?
'Tis full three months since I did see him last.
If any plague hang over us,[2] 't is he,
I would to God, my lords, he might be found.
Inquire at London, 'mongst the taverns there,
For there, they say, he daily doth frequent,[3]
With unrestrainéd, loose[4] companions,
Even such, they say, as stand in narrow lanes,
And beat our watch,[5] and rob our passengers;[6]
Which he, young wanton and effeminate boy,
Takes on the point of honour to support
So dissolute a crew.[7]

PERCY

My lord, some two days since I saw the prince,
And told him of those triumphs held at Oxford.

8 *gallant* – "fine young gentleman".

9 *would unto the stews* – "would go to the houses of common prostitutes ...".

10 *favour* – "sign of his lady's affection". A knight fighting in a tournament would wear a ribbon or glove given to him by a rich and noble lady whom he wished to marry.

11 *unhorse the lustiest challenger* – "knock down from his horse the youngest and strongest (*lustiest*) of those who entered the competition and called others to fight against them (*challenger*)".

12 *As dissolute ... forth* – "As bad in morals (*dissolute*) as he is wild (*desperate*) in courage, yet underneath (*through*) both these faults, I see some good in his character which later time may bring out to something better (*happily*)". (His sparks of good may blaze up into a fire.)

13 *conference* – "private talk".

And beat our watch[5]

BOLINGBROKE

And what said the gallant?[8]

PERCY

His answer was: he would unto the stews,[9]
And from the common'st creature pluck a glove
And wear it as a favour,[10] and with that
He would unhorse the lustiest challenger.[11]

BOLINGBROKE

As dissolute as desperate, yet through both,
I see some sparks of better hope which elder days
May happily bring forth.[12] But who comes here?

Enter AUMERLE *amazed*

AUMERLE

Where is the king?

BOLINGBROKE

What means our cousin, that he stares and looks
So wildly?

AUMERLE

God save your grace, I do beseech your majesty
To have some conference[13] with your grace alone.

BOLINGBROKE

Withdraw yourselves, and leave us here alone.

[*Exeunt* PERCY *and* Lords

What is the matter with our cousin now?

AUMERLE

[*Kneels*]
For ever may my knees grow to the earth,
My tongue cleave to my roof within my mouth,
Unless a pardon, ere I rise, or speak.

14 *If on the first . . . love* – "If your offence was planned only, and not carried out, then to gain your support in the future (*after*) . . .".

15 *safe* – "unable to harm me".

16 *secure* – "over-confident".

17 *Shall I . . . face?* – "Will you not allow me, out of my love for you, to speak to you face to face of this treason?"

BOLINGBROKE

Intended or committed was this fault?
If on the first, how heinous e'er it be,
To win thy after love,[14] I pardon thee.

AUMERLE

Then give me leave that I may turn the key,
That no man enter till my tale be done.

BOLINGBROKE

Have thy desire.

The DUKE OF YORK *knocks at the door and shouts*

YORK

My liege, beware; look to thyself!
Thou hast a traitor in thy presence there.

BOLINGBROKE

Villain, I'll make thee safe.[15] *[Draws his sword*

AUMERLE

Stay thy revengeful hand; thou hast no cause to fear.

YORK

Open the door, secure[16] fool-hardy king!
Shall I for love speak treason to thy face?[17]
Open the door, or I will break it open.

BOLINGBROKE *unlocks the door to let* YORK *in and locks it again*

BOLINGBROKE

What is the matter, uncle? Speak!
Recover breath; tell us how near is danger,
That we may arm us to encounter it.

18 *forbids me show* – "stops my explaining".

19 *My heart . . . hand* – "Although my signature (*hand*) is there, my feelings are not in league (*confederate*) with those who made the plot".

20 *begets* – "is the father, the cause, of".

21 *sheer* – "pure".

22 *From whence . . . himself.* York's loyal character is like a pure fountain, but his son Aumerle, the stream which flowed from this fountain (*From whence this stream Hath held his current*), running through channels (*passages*) of mud has become dirty (*defiled himself*). The *muddy passages* are his evil companions in this plot.

23 *Thy overflow . . . son* – "The son born (*overflow*) of a virtuous father (*of good*) has changed (*converts*) to something wicked, and your plentiful (*abundant*) good qualities shall gain pardon (*excuse*) for the crime (*blot*), which would otherwise be punished by death (*deadly*), in your son who has gone off the right road (*digressing*)".

24 *his vice's bawd* – "the wicked agent (*bawd*) who makes his sin possible".

25 *shall spend . . . gold* – "will throw away my good character in buying himself off the punishment for his own shame, just as wasteful (*thriftless*) sons spend the money their father has gathered together bit by bit".

26 *Mine honour . . . in his life.* York argues that his own honour is safe (*lives*) only if Aumerle is executed; York's life will be full of shame if his dishonoured son is allowed to live. If the king lets Aumerle live (*in his life*), York's good name dies (*Thou kill'st me*).

YORK

Peruse this writing here, and thou shalt know
The treason that my haste forbids me show.[18]

AUMERLE

Remember, as thou read'st, thy promise passed:
I do repent me; read not my name there.
My heart is not confederate with my hand.[19]

YORK

It was, villain, ere thy hand did set it down.
I tore it from the traitor's bosom, king.
Fear, and not love, begets[20] his penitence;
Forget to pity him, lest thy pity prove
A serpent, that will sting thee to the heart.

BOLINGBROKE

Oh heinous, strong, and bold conspiracy!
O loyal father of a treacherous son!
Thou sheer,[21] immaculate, and silver fountain,
From whence this stream, through muddy passages
Hath held his current, and defiled himself![22]
Thy overflow of good converts to bad,
And thy abundant goodness shall excuse
This deadly blot in thy digressing son.[23]

YORK

So shall my virtue be his vice's bawd;[24]
And he shall spend mine honour, with his shame,
As thriftless sons their scraping father's gold.[25]
Mine honour lives when his dishonour dies,
Or my shamed life in his dishonour lies:
Thou kill'st me in his life;[26] giving him breath,
The traitor lives, the true man 's put to death.

27 *This festered joint . . . confound* – "If you cut off this poisoned (*festered*) limb (*joint*), the remainder of the body (*rest*) will stay (*rest*) healthy (*sound*); if you leave this alone, it will destroy (*confound*) all the rest".

28 *Love loving . . . can* – "If he does not love his own family, his own son, how can he love his king?"

29 *what dost . . . rear* – "why (*what*) are you interfering (*make*) here? You nursed this traitor at your breast (*dugs*) when he was a helpless baby. Do you hope to nurse (*rear*) him to life again (*once more*) now that he has deserved to die?"

DUCHESS

[*Calling from outside*] What hoa, my liege! For God's sake, let me in!

BOLINGBROKE

What shrill-voiced suppliant makes this eager cry?

DUCHESS

A woman, and thy aunt, great king; 't is I.
Speak with me, pity me, open the door!
A beggar begs that never begged before.

BOLINGBROKE

Our scene is altered from a serious thing,
And now changed to "The Beggar and the King."
My dangerous cousin, let your mother in,
I know she is come to pray for your foul sin.

YORK

If thou do pardon whosoever pray,
More sins for this forgiveness prosper may;
This festered joint cut off, the rest rest sound;
This let alone will all the rest confound.[27]

Enter DUCHESS

DUCHESS

O king, believe not this hard-hearted man!
Love loving not itself none other can.[28]

YORK

Thou frantic woman, what dost thou make here?
Shall thy old dugs once more a traitor rear?[29]

30 *see day that the happy* – "look up to the daylight that the happy person . . .".

31 *Ill mayst . . . grace* – "I wish that things may turn out badly for you if you grant any kind of pardon!"

32 *but faintly . . . denied* – "only in a soft weak voice (*faintly*) and would like to be (*would be*) refused (*denied*)".

DUCHESS

Sweet York, be patient! Here me, gentle liege. [*Kneels*

BOLINGBROKE

Rise up, good aunt.

DUCHESS

Not yet, I thee beseech.
For ever will I walk upon my knees,
And never see day that the happy[30] sees
Till thou give joy, until thou bid me joy,
By pardoning Rutland, my transgressing boy.

AUMERLE

Unto my mother's prayers I bend my knee. [*Kneels*

YORK

Against them both my true joints bended be. [*Kneels*
Ill mayst thou thrive, if thou grant any grace![31]

DUCHESS

Pleads he in earnest? Look upon his face!
His eyes do drop no tears: his prayers are in jest:
His words come from his mouth, ours from our breast.
He prays but faintly and would be denied;[32]
We pray with heart, and soul, and all beside.
His weary joints would gladly rise, I know;
Our knees shall kneel till to the ground they grow.
His prayers are full of false hypocrisy,
Ours of true zeal, and deep integrity.
Our prayers do out-pray his; then let them have
That mercy, which true prayer ought to have.

33 *thy tongue to teach* – "teaching you how to speak".

34 *meet* – "suitable".

35 "*Pardonne moi*" – "I am very sorry (*but I have to refuse*)".

36 *set'st the word . . . word* – "make one word fight against the other".

37 *chopping* – "mincing, affected".

38 *Thine eye . . . rehearse* – "Your eyes are filling with sympathy or tears; let your tongue learn what to say from there; or listen to what your pitiful (*piteous*) heart is feeling, so that, when you hear how our laments (*plaints*) and prayers bring pain to your heart (*pierce*), pity may affect you to repeat (*rehearse*) the word 'Pardon' ".

39 *sue* – "beg".

40 *all the suit . . . hand* – "the only request I am making".

BOLINGBROKE

Good aunt, stand up.

DUCHESS

Nay, do not say "Stand up!"
Say "Pardon" first, and afterwards "Stand up."
And if I were thy nurse, thy tongue to teach,[33]
"Pardon" should be the first word of thy speech.
I never longed to hear a word till now:
Say "Pardon", king; let pity teach thee how.
The word is short: but not so short as sweet,
No word like "Pardon" for kings' mouths so meet.[34]

YORK

Speak it in French, king; say "Pardonne moi."[35]

DUCHESS

Dost thou teach pardon pardon to destroy?
Ah, my sour husband, my hard-hearted lord,
That set'st the word itself against the word.[36]
Speak "Pardon" as 't is current in our land;
The chopping[37] French we do not understand.
Thine eye begins to speak, set thy tongue there,
Or in thy piteous heart plant thou thine ear,
That hearing how our plaints and prayers do pierce,
Pity may move thee "Pardon" to rehearse.[38]

BOLINGBROKE

Good aunt, stand up.

DUCHESS

I do not sue[39] to stand,
Pardon is all the suit I have in hand.[40]

41 *happy vantage of* – "fortunate gain from . . .".

42 *twain* – "two".

43 *brother-in-law . . . heels* – "the Earl of Huntingdon, and the Abbot of Westminster and all the rest of that gang (*crew*) of conspirators (*consorted*), death at once (*straight*) shall follow and hunt them down (*dog them at the heels*)".

44 *powers* – "forces of soldiers".

BOLINGBROKE

I pardon him, as God shall pardon me.

DUCHESS

O happy vantage of[41] a kneeling knee:
Yet am I sick for fear. Speak it again,
Twice saying "Pardon" doth not pardon twain,[42]
But makes one pardon strong.

BOLINGBROKE

With all my heart
I pardon him.

DUCHESS

A god on earth thou art.

BOLINGBROKE

But for our trusty brother-in-law, the Abbot,
With all the rest of that consorted crew,
Destruction straight shall dog them at the heels.[43]
Good uncle, help to order several powers[44]
To Oxford, or where'er these traitors are.
They shall not live within this world, I swear,
But I will have them, if I once know where.
Uncle, farewell, and, cousin, too, adieu:
Your mother well hath prayed, and prove you true!

DUCHESS

Come, my old son; I pray God make thee new.

[*Exeunt*

(v.iv) Exton believes that he has heard Bolingbroke wishing that some good friend of his would kill Richard, who is imprisoned at Pomfret. Bolingbroke, he thinks, looked closely at him, as if wishing Exton would make him safer by killing his rival. This Exton is ready to do.

1 *mark* – "notice".
2 *will rid . . . fear?* – "who will free me from the fear I have as long as this man lives?"
3 *urged it* – "asked it very seriously".
4 *speaking it . . . man* – "as he spoke, he looked at me very closely (*wistly*), like someone who wanted to (*would*) say, 'I wish you were the man . . .'".
5 *divorce* – "take away".
6 *rid* – "destroy".

Scene IV.

Enter EXTON *and* Servants.

EXTON

Didst thou not mark[1] the king, what words he spake?
"Have I no friend will rid me of this living fear?"[2]
Was it not so?

SERVANT

These were his very words.

EXTON

"Have I no friend?" quoth he; he spake it twice,
And urged it[3] twice together, did he not?

SERVANT

He did.

EXTON

And speaking it, he wistly looked on me,
As who should say "I would thou wert the man[4]
That would divorce[5] this terror from my heart,"
Meaning the king at Pomfret. Come, let 's go;
I am the king's friend, and will rid[6] his foe.

[*Exeunt*

(v.v) Richard is alone in his prison room, and he wants to compare his prison to the world outside. His different thoughts seem to him like many different people and no one thought is satisfied, just as people are not. He thinks of heaven and wonders if he can hope to come there. Then he pretends that he might be able to escape from prison. He reminds himself that other men have suffered misfortune. Hearing music played and noticing the mistakes in the playing he remembers the mistakes he made as king. Now he is like a clock and the moving on of time brings him nearer to death. It seems that a poor groom has been playing for him – a boy who worked in his stables when he was king. He tells Richard how Bolingbroke rode through London on his coronation day on Richard's horse, Barbary, and how the horse seemed proud of its rider. As the gaoler comes in with Richard's food the groom is sent away. The gaoler refuses to taste the food as he usually does because of the orders of Sir Pierce of Exton. At the gaoler's cries, Exton and his men rush in; Richard snatches a sword from one of the men and kills two of the servants before he himself is murdered. Exton thinks that he has done an evil deed; he will take Richard's dead body to London to King Henry.

1 *beget . . . thoughts* – "bring forth as their children (*generation*) thoughts which are always (*still*) producing (*breeding*) other thoughts".

2 *In humours* – "all having different tempers (*humours*)".

3 *The better sort . . . needle's eye* – "The better kind of thoughts, as, for example, thoughts about God (*things divine*) are mingled (*intermixed*) with doubts (*scruples*) and quote one part of the Bible against another, as in this example; comparing the words which say that little children shall enter the kingdom of Heaven with the saying that it is easier for a camel to pass through (*thread*) the gate (*postern*) of a needle's eye than for a rich man to enter Heaven"..

4 *tending to* – "which have to do with".

5 *nails* – "finger nails".

6 *flinty ribs* – "hard stone framework of this castle (as the ribs are the framework of a man's chest)".

7 *ragged* – "rough".

8 *of fortune's slaves* – "to have been brought down by fortune to the greatest misery".

9 *stocks*, wooden framework in which a man's legs could be fastened as a legal punishment for some small offence, e.g. for begging without permission.

10 *refuge their shame . . . sit there* – "find refuge from their own disgrace in the idea that many people have sat there before them, and others will have to after them".

11 *of ease, . . . the like* – "of comfort, as if carrying (*Bearing*) the weight of their own troubles (*misfortunes*) not on their own backs, but on the backs of others who have suffered (*endured*) the same thing (*like*) before".

12 *Thus play I* – "In this way I act the part of . . .".

13 *treasons* – "thinking of treasons which can be plotted against a king".

Scene V. Pomfret Castle.

Enter RICHARD *alone.*

RICHARD

I have been studying how I may compare
This prison where I live unto the world:
And for because the world is populous
And here is not a creature but myself,
I cannot do it: yet I 'll hammer 't out.
My brain, I 'll prove the female to my soul,
My soul, the father; and these two beget
A generation of still-breeding thoughts;[1]
And these same thoughts people this little world
In humours[2] like the people of this world,
For no thought is contented. The better sort,
As thoughts of things divine, are intermixed
With scruples, and do set the word itself
Against the word, as thus; "Come little ones", and then again,
"It is as hard to come as for a camel
To thread the postern of a needle's eye."[3]
Thoughts tending to[4] ambition, they do plot
Unlikely wonders; how these vain, weak nails[5]
May tear a passage through the flinty ribs[6]
Of this hard world, my ragged[7] prison walls:
And for they cannot, die in their own pride.
Thoughts tending to content flatter themselves,
That they are not the first of fortune's slaves,[8]
Nor shall not be the last; like silly beggars,
Who, sitting in the stocks,[9] refuge their shame
That many have, and others must, sit there;[10]
And in this thought, they find a kind of ease,
Bearing their own misfortunes on the back
Of such as have before endured the like.[11]
Thus play I[12] in one person many people,
And none contented. Sometimes am I king;
Then treasons[13] make me wish myself a beggar,

14 *better* – "better off".
15 *But whate'er . . . being nothing* – "But whatever I imagine myself to be, neither I nor anyone else who is only a mortal man (*but man is*), can be satisfied with having no possessions and no position until he is comforted (*eased*) by death (*being nothing*)".
16 *sour* – "unpleasant".
17 *time is broke . . . kept* – "rhythm is broken and no order followed".
18 *here have I . . . broke* – "in listening to actual music (*here*) I have a fineness (*daintiness*) of ear to catch a mistake in rhythm (*time broke*) when a string is wrongly touched (*disordered*); but when it was a case of (*for*) being able to match (*concord*, "matching") my government of England (*state*) with the different needs of the time, I was not able to understand what mistakes I was making (*my true time broke*)".
19 *I wasted time . . . me* – "I used my time foolishly and now the passing of time is bringing me to the end of my life".
20 *his numbering clock* – "his clock for counting the passing of time".
21 *My thoughts are minutes . . . tears* – "Each minute I have a new thought (of sorrow); at every sigh I give, a minute jerks forward on the clock-face (*watch*) towards a new hour; the hours, marked on the outside (*outward*) edge of the clock-face (*watch*), are my eyes, and to them (*whereto*) my finger, like the hour hand (*a dial's point*) goes on pointing as it wipes away my tears" (*jar*, "to jerk").
22 *posting on, in* – "quickly forward, measuring . . .".
23 *jack o' the clock*, the figure of a little man (*jack*) which, in old clocks, struck the bell every quarter or every hour. Richard imagines himself waiting like a fool to strike his own last hour.
24 *mads* – "maddens".
25 *it have holp . . . wits* – "music has helped (*holp*) lunatics to recover their senses (*wits*) . . .".
26 *a strange brooch . . . world* – "an unusual (*strange*) ornament in this world where all men hate me".

Who, sitting in the stocks,[9] *refuge their shame*

And so I am. Then crushing penury,
Persuades me, I was better[14] when a king;
Then am I kinged again; and by and by,
Think that I am unkinged by Bolingbroke,
And straight am nothing. But whate'er I be,
Nor I, nor any man, that but man is,
With nothing shall be pleased, till he be eased
With being nothing.[15] [*Music*] Music do I hear?
Ha, ha! Keep time! How sour[16] sweet music is,
When time is broke, and no proportion kept![17]
So is it in the music of men's lives:
And here have I the daintiness of ear,
To hear time broke in a disordered string;
But for the concord of my state and time,
Had not an ear to hear my true time broke.[18]
I wasted time, and now doth time waste me;[19]
For now hath time made me his numbering clock.[20]
My thoughts are minutes; and with sighs they jar
Their watches on unto mine eyes, the outward watch,
Whereto my finger, like a dial's point,
Is pointing still, in cleansing them from tears.[21]
Now, sir, the sounds that tell what hour it is
Are clamorous groans, which strike upon my heart,
Which is the bell; so sighs and tears and groans
Show minutes, times, and hours; but my time
Runs posting on, in[22] Bolingbroke's proud joy,
While I stand fooling here, his jack o' the clock.[23]
This music mads[24] me! Let it sound no more!
For though it have holp madmen to their wits,[25]
In me it seems, it will make wise men mad.
Yet blessing on his heart that gives it me!
For 't is a sign of love, and love to Richard
Is a strange brooch in this all-hating world.[26]

Enter Groom

27 *peer.* This word has two meanings, "lord" and "equal". If Richard is now to be called a *royal prince,* then the poor boy who gives him that title could just as well be called a *noble lord.* But, Richard suggests, the two of them are really equal, and he makes a joke about the value of two coins, the *royal* and the *noble.* A "royal" is worth 50p., a "noble" 33½p. For the groom to call Richard (*the cheapest of us*) a *royal* is to make Richard ten groats (16½p.) too dear; (the "*groat*", another coin, was worth 1½p.).

28 *ado . . . face* – "trouble at last got permission to see one who was once (*sometimes*) my royal master".

29 *yearned* – "grieved".

30 *bestrid* – "sat astride".

31 *dressed* – "groomed".

32 *How went he under him?* – "How did the horse behave when Bolingbroke was on his back?"

33 *jade* – "worthless horse".

his jack o' the clock[23]

GROOM

Hail, royal prince!

RICHARD

Thanks, noble peer.[27]
The cheapest of us is ten groats too dear.
What art thou? And how com'st thou hither
Where no man never comes, but that sad dog
That brings me food, to make misfortune live?

GROOM

I was a poor groom of thy stable, king,
When thou wert king; who, travelling towards York,
With much ado at length have gotten leave
To look upon my sometimes royal master's face.[28]
O how it yearned[29] my heart, when I beheld
In London streets, that coronation day,
When Bolingbroke rode on roan Barbary,
That horse that thou so often hast bestrid,[30]
That horse that I so carefully have dressed.[31]

RICHARD

Rode he on Barbary? Tell me, gentle friend,
How went he under him?[32]

GROOM

So proudly, as if he disdained the ground.

RICHARD

So proud, that Bolingbroke was on his back!
That jade[33] hath eat bread from my royal hand,
This hand hath made him proud with clapping him.
Would he not stumble? Would he not fall down,
Since pride must have a fall, and break the neck
Of that proud man that did usurp his back?

34 *awed by man . . . bear* – "tamed and controlled (*awed*) by man were born to carry (*bear*) riders".

35 *burden . . . Bolingbroke* – "load like a stupid ass, pricked on with spurs, rubbed sore (*galled*) and tired by prancing (*jauncing*) Bolingbroke".

36 *Keeper* – "gaoler".

37 *give place . . . stay* – "get away; you cannot stay here any longer".

38 *fall to* – "eat".

39 *wont* – "accustomed" (for fear of poison).

40 *stale* – "grown old and dry (as, for example, bread grows stale)".

GROOM: Hail, royal prince!
RICHARD: Thanks, noble peer.[27]

Forgiveness, horse! Why do I rail on thee,
Since thou, created to be awed by man,
Wast born to bear?[34] I was not made a horse,
And yet I bear a burden like an ass,
Spurred, galled, and tired by jauncing Bolingbroke.[35]

Enter Keeper[36] *with a dish*

KEEPER

Fellow, give place; here is no longer stay.[37]

RICHARD

If thou love me, 't is time thou wert away.

GROOM

What my tongue dares not, that my heart shall say. [*Exit*

KEEPER

My lord, will 't please you to fall to?[38]

RICHARD

Taste of it first, as thou art wont[39] to do.

KEEPER

My lord, I dare not: Sir Pierce of Exton who lately came from the king, commands the contrary.

RICHARD

The devil take Henry of Lancaster, and thee;
Patience is stale,[40] and I am weary of it.

KEEPER

Help, help, help!

Enter EXTON *and* Servants, *armed*

41 *What means death . . . assault?* – "Who is to be killed in this fierce (*rude*) attack (*assault*)?"
42 *room* – "place".
43 *never-quenching fire* – "fire which shall never be put out (*quench*)".
44 *staggers thus my person* – "makes me move so unsteadily".
45 *seat* – "place, throne".
46 *gross flesh* – "earthly and sinful body".
47 *spilled.* "Spill" has two meanings, "to shed" and "to destroy". Exton has put an end to the king's courage (*valour*) in shedding his blood.
48 *devil* – "evil spirit in my mind".
49 *chronicled* – "written down as part of history".

(v.vi) At Windsor Castle Bolingbroke is waiting for news of the rebellion against him. Northumberland tells him that four of the leaders have been captured and executed; their heads have been sent to London. Fitzwater announces that two of those who plotted to kill Bolingbroke when he was at Oxford have been put to death. Another member of the plot, the Abbot of Westminster, has died; a fourth, the Bishop of Carlisle, has his life spared by Bolingbroke. The coffin of Richard is carried in, but Bolingbroke will not thank Exton for the murder he has done; no reward but banishment is given him. Bolingbroke orders that the nobles mourn for Richard; he intends to go on a pilgrimage to the Holy Land to free himself of his guilt.

1 *consumed with fire* – "burned down, destroyed"
2 *ta'en or slain* – "captured or killed".

RICHARD

How now? What means death in this rude assault?[41]
Villain, thy own hand yields thy death's instrument!
[*Snatches a weapon from a* Servant *and strikes him down*
Go thou and fill another room[42] in hell.
[*He kills another.* EXTON *strikes him down*
That hand shall burn in never-quenching fire,[43]
That staggers thus my person,[44] Exton, thy fierce hand,
Hath with the king's blood stained the king's own land.
Mount, mount, my soul! Thy seat[45] is up on high,
Whilst my gross flesh[46] sinks downward, here to die. [*Dies*

EXTON

As full of valour as of royal blood!
Both have I spilled.[47] Oh would the deed were good!
For now the devil[48] that told me I did well,
Says that this deed is chronicled[49] in hell.
This dead king to the living king I 'll bear,
Take hence the rest, and give them burial here.
[*Exeunt*

Scene VI. Windsor Castle.

Flourish. Enter BOLINGBROKE, YORK, *with other* Lords *and* Attendants.

BOLINGBROKE

Kind uncle York, the latest news we hear
Is that the rebels have consumed with fire[1]
Our town of Cicester in Gloucestershire,
But whether they be ta'en or slain[2] we hear not.

Enter NORTHUMBERLAND

Welcome, my lord. What is the news?

3 *The manner . . . discourséd* – "how they were captured may be seen described (*discourséd*) at length (*large*) . . .".

4 *thy pains . . . gains* – "your efforts (*pains*), and shall repay your merit (*worth*) with rewards which you have truly deserved (*right worthy*)".

5 *consorted traitors . . . overthrow* – "traitors in the plot together (*consorted*) who intended (*sought*) to bring about for you at Oxford a fearful (*dire*) fall from power (*overthrow*)".

6 *wot* – "know".

7 *grand* – "chief".

8 *clog* – "heavy weight (such as might be fastened to an animal to stop its moving)".

9 *to abide . . . doom* – "to hear and suffer (*abide*) your royal judgement".

10 *some reverend room . . . strife* – "some holy (*reverend*) place (*room*) bigger (*More*) than the prison you have, and in it enjoy your life: so long as you live without rebelling in the future, you shall live out your life without attack (*strife*) from me".

NORTHUMBERLAND

First, to thy sacred state wish I all happiness:
The next news is I have to London sent
The heads of Oxford, Salisbury, Blunt, and Kent:
The manner of their taking may appear
At large discourséd[3] in this paper here.

BOLINGBROKE

We thank thee, gentle Percy, for thy pains,
And to thy worth will add right worthy gains.[4]

Enter FITZWATER

FITZWATER

My lord, I have from Oxford sent to London
The heads of Brocas, and Sir Bennet Seely,
Two of the dangerous consorted traitors
That sought at Oxford thy dire overthrow.[5]

BOLINGBROKE

Thy pains, Fitzwater, shall not be forgot;
Right noble is thy merit, well I wot.[6]

Enter PERCY *and the* BISHOP OF CARLISLE

PERCY

The grand[7] conspirator, Abbot of Westminster,
With clog[8] of conscience and sour melancholy
Hath yielded up his body to the grave;
But here is Carlisle living, to abide
Thy kingly doom[9] and sentence of his pride.

BOLINGBROKE

Carlisle, this is your doom:
Choose out some secret place, some reverend room
More than thou hast, and with it joy thy life:
So as thou liv'st in peace, die free from strife:[10]

11 *Thy buried fear* – "what you once feared, now ready for burial".

12 *wrought A deed . . . head* – "done (*wrought*) an act with your murderous (*fatal*) hand which will make people speak evil (*slander*) about me . . .".

13 *From your own mouth* – "Acting on your own words . . .".

14 *Cain.* In Biblical story Cain became an outcast as God's punishment for his murder of his brother Abel.

15 *thorough,* "through".

16 *protest* – "declare".

17 *That blood . . . grow* – "that I should become powerful through murder" (as a plant grows when it is sprinkled with water).

18 *that* – "what".

19 *sullen black incontinent* – "gloomy black clothes at once (*incontinent*)".

20 *voyage* – "journey, pilgrimage".

21 *after . . . bier* – "behind me, join me in doing honour (*grace*) to the dead man by mourning, following (*after*) with tears the bier of one who died too soon (*untimely*)"; (*bier,* "a framework on which the coffin was carried").

Enter EXTON, with persons bearing a coffin

For though mine enemy thou hast ever been,
High sparks of honour in thee have I seen.

Enter EXTON, *with persons bearing a coffin*

EXTON

Great king, within this coffin I present
Thy buried fear.[11] Herein all breathless lies
The mightiest of thy greatest enemies,
Richard of Bordeaux, by me hither brought.

BOLINGBROKE

Exton, I thank thee not, for thou hast wrought
A deed of slander, with thy fatal hand,
Upon my head[12] and all this famous land.

EXTON

From your own mouth,[13] my lord, did I this deed.

BOLINGBROKE

They love not poison that do poison need,
Nor do I thee: though I did wish him dead,
I hate the murderer, love him murderéd.
The guilt of conscience take thou for thy labour,
But neither my good word, nor princely favour.
With Cain[14] go wander thorough[15] shades of night,
And never show thy head by day nor light.
Lords, I protest,[16] my soul is full of woe,
That blood should sprinkle me to make me grow.[17]
Come mourn with me for that[18] I do lament,
And put on sullen black incontinent.[19]
I 'll make a voyage[20] to the Holy-land,
To wash this blood off from my guilty hand.
March sadly after, grace my mournings here,
In weeping after this untimely bier.[21]

[*Exeunt*

GLOSSARY

This glossary explains all the words in the play which are used in Modern English as they were in Shakespeare's day, but which are not among the 3,000 most-used words in the language.

The notes opposite the text explain words or meanings which are *not* used in Modern English. In these notes it has been necessary to use a very few words which are also outside the 3,000-word list; these are included in the glossary.

Explanations in the glossary are given entirely within the chosen list of words.

Only the meaning of the word as used in the play or in the notes is normally given.

n. = "noun"; v. = "verb"; adj. = "adjective"; p.t. = "past tense"; p.pt. = "past participle".

A

abbot, head of a place where religious men live apart, and of their church.
abet, to help in doing something bad.
abstain, *a. from*, to keep away from.
accent, special weight given by the voice to one part of a word.
accomplice, companion in wrong-doing.
achieve, to gain.
adder, small poisonous snake.
ado, trouble and excitement.
adversary, enemy.
aggravate, to make worse.
ague, fever.
aid, help.
allegiance, loyalty, duty to one's ruler.
ambush, hiding of men in a secret place so as to make a surprise attack.
ancestor(s), those persons from whom one is descended, e.g. great-great-grandfather, etc.
anoint, to make holy by putting oil on. (A king is anointed at the ceremony of his crowning.)
apparent, clear to see.
armour, iron covering to protect against weapons.
arrest, to stop, seize (often by officer of the law).
ascend, to go up (on to).
aspect, sight.
assign, to fix a time for, appoint.

assure, to make certain.
awe, feeling of respect and fear.
awry, bent to one side, not straight.

B

bait, to set upon (a person or animal) so as to make angry.
balcony, upstairs part of a theatre.
balm, oily liquid.
banish, to send from one's own country as a punishment.
bankrupt, unable to pay one's debts.
barbarian, a man without laws, manners or good customs.
bark, skin on the outside of a tree.
barren, having no fruit, children or young; useless.
bastard, a child whose parents were not married; not real.
battlement, wall on the top of a castle.
beget, to cause to be born, produce.
begot, p.t. of *beget*.
beguile, to deceive.
bequeath, to give or pass on to others after death.
bereave, to take away.
bereft, p.pt. of *bereave*.
beseech, to ask anxiously and eagerly.
bile, bitter, yellow-green liquid which changes fatty food in the body into a form in which it can be used by the body; bad temper.
bishop, high officer in the Church.
boisterous, wild, noisy.
boon, favour.
borne, carried.
bounce, (of a ball) to spring up again from the ground.
bounty, generosity.
brace, *a b. of*, two.
brandish, to wave (a sword) about.
brazen, made of brass.
brief, short.
brittle, hard and easily broken like glass.

C

calamity, any cause that produces great evil.
capital, punishable by death.
carpet, thick floor-covering.
casement, window which opens like a door.
cast, to throw.
challenge, call to fight.
champion, one who fights for some other person or for some good cause.
charter, written paper from the king or state giving certain rights.
chastise, to punish.
cherish, to care for, protect.
chide, to blame for a fault.
clamorous, very noisy.
cleave, to stick (to).
clergyman, priest of the Church of England.
cloak, loose outer garment.
clog, to cause difficulty in moving.
cloister, place where men or women live lives of study and prayer apart from the world.
combat, to fight.
compassion, feeling of pity for sorrows of others.
comprise, to contain, be made up of.
compromise, agreement.
conceal, to hide.
concentrate, *to c. on*, to give one's whole mind to.
confederate, joined by agreement for a common purpose.
consent, to agree.

conspiracy, secret plan to do an unlawful act.
contact, touch.
contempt, scorn.
contrast, very noticeable difference.
contrive, to plan cleverly.
convey, to carry, take.
courtesy, politeness.
covenant, solemn promise or agreement.
cradle, bed for a small baby which can be rocked from side to side.
craft, cunning.
craftsman, workman.
crave, to ask eagerly for.
crest, a sign which serves as the special mark of a family.
crimson, deep red.

D

dainty, a specially nice piece of food.
dangle, to hang down and swing loosely.
dash, to throw with force.
dearth, famine, serious lack of food.
debase, to make of less value.
deceitful, deceiving.
decree, to command as king.
deem, to judge, think.
degenerate, grown into a very bad character.
delectable, full of enjoyment.
denounce, to speak against.
depose, to put down from some high office, e.g. from being king.
deputy, one who is given power to act for another.
desolate, sad and lonely.
desperate, ready for any wild act.
detest, to hate.
devise, to invent, imagine.
devour, to eat up greedily.
dice, small six-sided piece of bone or wood, with one to six spots on each side, used for games of chance.
digest, to change what is eaten so that it can be taken into the blood.
dire, terrible.
disdain, to look down upon with scorn.
dismal, cheerless, sorrowful.
dispatch, to send off quickly.
disperse, to break up, disband.
dissolve, to make a solid or gas become liquid by putting it into liquid, to melt.
divine (adj.) having to do with God.
divine (v.) to guess what is to come.
divorce, separation of man and wife by court of law.
dramatis personae (Latin), "the people of the drama", list of characters in the play.
dramatist, writer of a play.

E

effeminate, (of men) behaving like a woman, lacking in courage.
emphasise, to give special force (to).
energy, force, strength.
enmity, state of being an enemy.
ensign, flag.
ensue, to follow.
entitle, to give a name to.
entreat, to beg.
epitaph, that which is written on a stone above a grave.
evidence, anything that helps to prove a fact.
execute, to put to death by order of the law.
executor, person appointed to do what is written in a dead person's will.

exeunt, Latin word for "(they) go out".
exile, punishment of being sent out of one's own country.
exit, Latin word for "he (she) goes out"
expire, to die, end.
external having to do with the outside.
extinct, dead.
extravagance, spending money foolishly.

F

faction, side.
falcon, bird trained to hunt other birds.
falter, to speak or walk unsteadily.
fawn, *f. upon*, to flatter like a dog.
fealty, loyalty to a king or ruler.
fell, to cut down.
fertile, producing much.
fester, (of a wound) to become poisoned.
fiend, evil and cruel spirit.
figured, patterned.
financier, one who controls a large amount of money.
font, stone container for the holy water which is put on a child when he is baptised (i.e. named and accepted as a member of the church).
foolhardy, going into unnecessary danger.
forbear, to keep oneself from doing a certain action.
forefather, a person from whom one is descended.
foretell, to announce before it happens.
forge, to make so as to deceive; to make an iron instrument in a fire.
forgo, to be without, give up.
forswear, to promise not to use any more; to declare as true that which one knows to be untrue.
fortress, large castle or strong place.
forward, too eager.
foster, to nurse.
fountain, water coming up out of the ground.
frantic, mad or wildly excited.
fret, to wear away by rubbing.
frivolous, not serious, foolish.

G

gaoler, prison-guard.
gauntlet, glove. *To throw down the gauntlet* = to show that one is ready to fight.
gild, to cover with thin gold.
glossary, list of difficult words, with notes explaining them.
goblet, splendid drinking vessel.
gore, to wound, as a cow does with its horns.
gorgeous, very fine and beautiful.
graft, to attach part of a plant to another plant so that it lives and grows there.
grievous, very serious.
grin, to give a wide smile.
groom, servant in charge of horses.
ground, reason.

H

hack, to cut roughly with many blows.
hail, expression of welcome and respect.
handsome, good-looking (of a man).
harp, a musical instrument having many strings, played by touching the strings with the fingers.

haven, harbour.
headlong, head-first.
heinous, very bad (of an unlawful act).
helmet, iron covering to protect the head when fighting.
herald, officer who declares important news or who has to do with the signs painted on shields.
herb, plant used for medicine or for giving a special taste.
hermitage, place where a man lives a holy life apart from the world.
high, *h. treason*, attempt to harm the king.
horror, great fear and dislike.
household, family, all those living in one house.
Humber, estuary on the north-east coast of England (estuary = broad river mouth into which the sea flows).
hurl, to throw with great force.
hypocrisy, the act of pretending to have goodness and strength of character which one does not possess.

I

immaculate, pure, without fault.
impartial, not favouring one side, just.
impeach, to charge with disloyalty, to bring before a court of law on this charge.
impregnable, able to be defended against all attacks.
impress, to press upon the mind.
impute, to consider as belonging (to).
indignation, anger, usually at some just cause.
inevitable, which must happen, allowing no escape.
insinuate, to push oneself forward gently and secretly.
inspired, filled with great thoughts from God.
integrity, honesty.
intellect, power of mind by which we think and know.
intelligence, collecting of news.
ire, anger.

J

jest, to do or say what will produce laughter.

K

kindred, family of which one is a member.
kinsman, relative, member of one's family.
knight, a man of noble rank.

L

lagging, following slowly and unwillingly.
lament, to show great grief.
lance, spear used by horse-soldiers.
lease, to rent.
leave, to take l., to say good-bye.
leopard, a meat-eating animal, yellow with black spots, found in the forests of India and Africa.
levy, to raise money, raise an army.
lief, I had as l., I would like as much to.
likeness, A good likeness = a good picture of a person.
lime, white powder mixed with sand to make mortar (used for holding together the bricks and stones of a building).
liquor, a liquid.

literally, according to the actual meaning of the words.
loam, good soil.
loath, unwilling.
lop, to cut away.
lot, *my l.*, my fate.
lour, to look angry and threatening.
lunatic, mad.
lurk, to lie in wait.
lusty, young and strong.

M

maintain, to support, speak strongly in favour of.
man, to supply a place, which is to be defended, with men.
manor, a certain amount of land.
manure, to spread matter on the ground so as to give food to plants.
marshal, high officer of the king's court.
melancholy, feeling of great sadness.
meteor, a falling star.
metre, regular arrangement of sounds in poetry.
midwife, woman who helps women in childbirth.
misinterpret, to understand wrongly.
mislead, to lead to wrong actions.
mould, a hollow form into which liquid, (e.g. hot metal) is poured.
mount, to climb, get on to a horse.
muster, to gather together.
mutiny, rising against officers or rulers.

N

nettle, plant which, when touched, causes pain and redness of the skin.
neutral, taking neither side in a war.
nimble, quick of movement.
nunnery, a house for nuns (women living a life given to God).

O

oath, promise or declaration calling on the name of God.
object, *to o. against*, to bring as a charge against.
obscure, hidden, not well-known.
obtain, to get.
occident, west.
occur, to happen, be found.
omnipotent, all-powerful.
opponent, person who takes the other side in a fight.
outcast, homeless, friendless person.
outrage, very wrong or cruel act which causes great anger.
overtake, to come up level with a person from behind.
oyster, a flat shell-fish.

P

pace, step, speed.
pagan, a person who is not a Christian.
pageant, fine show or public performance.
parasite, a plant or animal which joins on to another and lives on its food or blood; a person who lives at another's cost.
parchment, animal skin used for writing on.
pasture, grass-land for cattle.
pawn, to get money by leaving an article of value which will be given back when the money is repaid.
peer, nobleman.

penalty, punishment.
penance, punishment or suffering given to oneself as a sign of sorrow for wrongdoing.
penitence, sorrow for wrong done.
penury, state of being very poor.
pernicious, harmful.
peruse, to read carefully.
pestilence, dangerous disease which spreads widely.
pilgrimage, journey to a holy place.
pine (n.), tree with needle-like leaves and soft white wood.
pine (v.), to waste away with grief.
pious, loving to serve God.
plate, gold and silver dishes.
plot, small piece of land.
pluck, to pull (off).
pomp, solemn ceremonial show.
populous, having many people in it.
prance, to jump along.
prattle, continous talk, like a child's.
presage, sign of a future event.
procure, to obtain.
prodigal, wasteful.
profane, to turn something holy to an evil use.
prophet, one who tells the future.
prostitute, woman who sells herself.
protest, to say that a thing should not be done.
proverb, short, wise saying.
provoke, to make angry, cause (through anger).
prune, to cut off parts of a tree to make it grow better.
punctuate, to put the stops (, ; : . etc.) into writing.
pun, a play on words, e.g. Those who make *puns* should be *pun*ished.
puny, small and weak.
purchase, to buy.

Q

quote, to repeat the words of another person saying whose words they are.

R

rancour, deep-rooted, unforgiving hatred.
range, limits.
ravenous, very hungry.
realm, kingdom.
rebuke, to find fault with, to blame.
recant, to say that one no longer believes in a former opinion.
recompense, reward.
reconcile, to make friendly again.
recover, to get back again.
redeem, to pay off a debt (as Christ redeemed the sins of men).
redemption, redeeming.
redress, setting right.
regal, of a king.
regalia, crown, sceptre and other ornaments of a king at his coronation.
regenerate, born again.
regent, ruler during the king's absence.
remiss, careless, not attending to duty.
repeal, to make (a law) of no further force.
repent, to feel sorry for having done (wrong).
residence, house.
revel, to feast merrily.
revenue, money coming in, e.g. to the government.
reverence, feeling of great respect.
reverend, worthy of great respect.
revolt, to rise against the king.

rhythm, regular beat of poetry, music, or dancing.
roan, a horse of brown colour.
rosary, a string of beads used for counting the number of prayers said.
rue, to be sorry (for).
ruffian, a rough, lawless fellow.

S

sacrament, bread and wine representing the body and blood of Christ.
safeguard, to protect.
salute, to greet.
sap, liquid in a plant.
scandal, action which causes an evil report.
sceptre, ornamental bar of gold held in his hand by a king.
scoff, to speak bitter words and to laugh at a person.
scowl, to look angrily.
section, part cut off.
sepulchre, grave cut in stone.
sequence, *s. of events*, a chain of events, one following after another.
serpent, snake.
sheath, case for a sword.
shiver, to shake with cold or fear.
shrill, high and loud.
shrink, to draw back from a dangerous or unpleasant thing.
siege, *to lay s. to a town*, to keep an army round it and attack it so as to take it.
sieve, a round frame with a wire net at the bottom, used for separating small things from large.
slander, untrue report spoken to damage another's character.
slaughter, to kill in large numbers.
slay, to kill.
slew, p. t. of *slay*.
sluice, to let flow through the door of a waterway.
socket, hollow in which something turns, e.g. eye-socket.
soothe, to calm an excited person.
sound, to measure the depth of water, to question.
sovereign, king.
spear, metal point fixed to a long stick used as a weapon.
spider, an 8-legged creature which lives in a fine net and eats flies.
spur, sharp point on the heel of a rider for pricking a horse to make it go fast.
stable, house in which horses or cattle are kept.
statute, law.
stewardship, office of looking after food and living arrangements of a large house.
stray, to wander from the right road.
stress, to say with special force.
stride, long step.
stumble, to make a wrong step and fall forward.
substitute, person appointed in place of another.
succession, (of persons or things) one coming after another.
sullen, silent and angry.
summons, order to a person to come at a certain time.
superfluous, more than necessary.
suppliant, one who prays for a favour.
surety, one who promises to make sure that another does as ordered.
surmount, to exceed.

surrender, to yield.
swift, rapid.
syllables, separate sound-groups into which a word can be divided.

T

taper, a very thin candle.
tapestry, a large cloth wall-hanging whose threads make a picture.
task, a piece of work which must be done.
tavern, drinking place, inn.
tedious, long and uninteresting.
tempest, great storm.
tenement, what is held by a tenant.
terrestrial, of this earth.
thrive, to be successful.
thrust, to push suddenly and with force.
tidings, news.
toad, frog-like creature, often looked on as a type of something hateful.
torment, to cause great pain.
torture, to cause great pain.
tradition, old custom.
traitor, one who harms his king or country by helping an enemy.
trample, to walk over and press down with the feet.
transfer, to move from one place to another.
transform, to change.
treachery, disloyalty.
treason, disloyalty to king or government.
trim, to make neat.
troop, crowd of people.
truce, an arrangement to stop a battle for a time.
tuft, a number of plants growing close together.
tumult, excitement and noise.
tutor, to teach.
twofold, double.

U

undertake, to take a duty on oneself.
unreverent, showing no respect.
unruly, unwilling to obey.
unseasonable, occurring out of season, at the wrong time of the year.
unwieldy, too large to be handled easily.
usurp, to seize by force and without right.

V

vagabond, homeless wanderer.
valour, great courage.
vassal, subject of a lord or a king.
vaunt, to talk proudly.
vellum, fine white skin of an animal prepared for writing on.
venom, poison.
verge, edge.
vex, to trouble, make angry.
vial, small glass bottle.
villain, wrong-doer.
viol, stringed musical instrument.
violate, to treat a holy thing with disrespect, to break.
viper, poisonous snake.
vivid, full of life.

W

wager, a promise that A will pay B if a certain thing happens, and B will pay A if it does not happen.
wail, to cry out with grief.
wallow, to roll about with enjoyment.

waver, to move unsteadily.
Welsh, of Wales.
wholesome, good for the health.
wilderness, desert.
withstand, to resist.
womb, part of the body in which the unborn child lives and grows.
wrinkle, small fold in surface of material, e.g. on the face of an old man.

Z

zeal, eagerness.

HINTS TO EXAMINATION CANDIDATES

This section is intended to offer some help to candidates who are studying *Richard II* for School Certificate or General Certificate of Education (Ordinary Level) examinations, and who are working alone. Actual questions from Cambridge and London papers are used as examples to show the kinds of question that may be found on most papers for examinations at this stage.

You will see first that you must know the story of the play in some detail. Secondly, you must give yourself practice in reading the questions carefully and answering exactly what is asked; do not expect to find on any paper a question that you have already answered. Thirdly, you must train yourself to write quickly enough to finish the work in the time allowed (30 minutes for each of these sample questions).

See to it that you know beforehand which kinds of question you *must* do and which you *may* do. For some examinations (e.g. London) you must do one 'context' question and you may also do an essay question on the set play; for others (e.g. Cambridge) you may have a choice between 'context' and essay questions.

"CONTEXT" QUESTIONS

1. (Cambridge University, Oversea School Certificate, December 1957). Choose THREE of the passages (*a*)–(*d*) and answer *briefly* the questions which follow:

(*a*) *Marshal.* The appellant in all duty greets your Highness,
And craves to kiss your hand and take his leave.
K. Rich. We will descend and fold him in our arms.
Cousin of Hereford, as thy cause is right,
So be thy fortune in this royal fight!
Farewell, my blood; which if today thou shed,
Lament we may, but not revenge thee dead.

(i) Who is the "appellant", where is he, and what is his claim?
(ii) How does this "royal fight" end?
(iii) Give in your own words the meaning of lines 6 and 7 (Farewell, my blood . . . dead).

(*b*) *A.* For us to levy power
Proportionable to the enemy
Is all unpossible.
B. Besides, our nearness to the King in love
Is near the hate of those love not the King.
C. And that is the wavering commons.

(i) Give the names of the three people taking part in this conversation. Who is "the enemy"?
(ii) Give in your own words the meaning of the 4th and 5th lines ("Besides . . . the King").
(iii) How does York later describe the behaviour of "the commons" to Richard on his entry into London?

(*c*) *Berkeley.* My Lord of Hereford, my message is to you.
Bolingbroke. My lord, my answer is – "to Lancaster";
And I am come to seek that name in England;
And I must find that title in your tongue
Before I make reply to aught you say.

(i) On what occasion did this interchange take place? Give the names of TWO other lords accompanying Bolingbroke at this time.
(ii) What does Bolingbroke mean by this reply, and how does he later justify his return to England?
(iii) What was the message brought by Berkeley, and who had sent it?

(*d*) *Duchess.* Pleads he in earnest? Look upon his face;
His eyes do drop no tears, his prayers are in jest;
His words come from his mouth, ours from our breast.
He prays but faintly and would be denied;
We pray the heart and soul, and all beside.

(i) To whom is the Duchess speaking? To whom is she referring when she says "he" and "we"?
(ii) For what is "he" praying, and why? Why does the Duchess say his prayers are in jest?

(iii) For what is the Duchess herself pleading? What answer does she receive to her prayers?

ANSWER

(*a*)

(i) Bolingbroke, in the lists at Coventry, claims that Mowbray is a traitor.

(ii) Richard stops the fight beginning and banishes Mowbray for life and Bolingbroke for six years.

(iii) Good-bye, Bolingbroke, my close relation; if in this fight today you are killed, I may grieve for your death, but justice will not let me take revenge, even though you are my cousin.

(*b*)

(i) Bushy, Green and Bagot. Bolingbroke.

(ii) In addition to this, the closeness of our friendship with the king makes us hated by those who dislike him.

(iii) They threw dust on to his sacred head.

(*c*)

(i) When Bolingbroke came to Berkeley Castle to meet York, governor of England in Richard's absence. Northumberland, Ross.

(ii) When he was banished his father was living; he has come now to claim his inheritance. He has come only for that.

(iii) Why had Bolingbroke landed with an army while Richard was in Ireland? York.

(*Notes:* A good deal of accurate information is necessary here. Write as simply and shortly as possible. Number the sections carefully. See that you have not left out any of the "bits" e.g. (*b*) (i) . . . Bolingbroke; (*c*) (iii) . . . York.

For (*a*) (iii) and (*b*) (ii) try out your sentence in pencil first. Your final attempt should be clearly written, without any crossings-out.

For (*c*) (i) be careful not to give the answer you will need for (*c*) (iii).)

2. (London University, G.C.E., Ordinary Level, Autumn 1956). Choose ONE of the following passages and answer the questions below it:

Either: (i)

Green. Well, he is gone; and with him go these thoughts.
Now for the rebels, which stand out in Ireland,
Expedient manage must be made my liege,
Ere further leisure yield them further means
For their advantage, and your Highness' loss.
K. Richard. We will ourself in person to this war,
And for our coffers with too great a Court
And liberal largess are grown somewhat light,
We are enforced to farm our royal realm.

(*a*) To whom does Green refer in line 1 and why has he "gone"?
(*b*) What are "these thoughts" mentioned by Green (line 1)?
(*c*) Give in your own words the meaning of lines 4 and 5 (*Ere further leisure . . . Highness' loss*).
(*d*) Give the meaning in this passage of *largess* (line 8) and *farm* (line 9).
(*e*) Mention two other methods, referred to in the play, which Richard adopted to raise money.

Or: (ii)

Duchess of York. The word is short, but not so short as sweet;
No word like pardon for kings' mouths so meet.
York. Speak it in French, King, say, pardonne moi.
Duchess of York. Dost thou teach pardon pardon to destroy?
Ah my sour husband, my hard-hearted lord,
That set'st the word itself against the word!
Speak pardon as 'tis current in our land,
The chopping French we do not understand.
Thine eye begins to speak, set thy tongue there.

(*a*) On whose behalf and for what offence is the Duchess asking for pardon?
(*b*) Bring out clearly the point of York's remark in line 3 (*Speak it in French . . . moi*).
(*c*) Give in your own words the meaning of line 6 (*That set'st . . . the word!*)
(*d*) Give in your own words the meaning of line 9 (*Thine eye . . . tongue there*).
(*e*) What is York's attitude towards the same offender when he first discovers the offence?

ANSWER

(i)

(*a*) To Bolingbroke; he has been banished from England for six years by King Richard.

(*b*) Richard had noticed with dislike how Bolingbroke took trouble to make himself popular with the common people as if he were the next heir to the throne.

(*c*) before they have more time and more opportunity to make themselves stronger and to weaken the power of the English king.

(*d*) generosity; to get money in advance from rich men in return for giving them the right to gather taxes.

(*e*) His deputies would force rich men to sign blank cheques and later they would fill in the sum of money to be paid; Richard made the nobles pay fines for what, he said, they had done wrong some years ago.

(*Notes:* Attempt one passage only. Number the sections carefully. You will see that you must know the play very well to be able to answer these detailed questions.

(*c*) requires a neatly arranged answer which will make clear, by rewording, the meaning of the given sentence. Try out your attempt in pencil first; your final version should be written out clearly without any crossings-out.)

ESSAY QUESTIONS

3. Describe briefly the part taken in *Richard II* by each of the two uncles of the king, the Duke of Lancaster and the Duke of York. What similarities and what differences do you find in the two men? (Cambridge University, Oversea School Certificate, December 1957.)

4. Illustrating your remarks by close reference to their speeches and actions, write character-sketches of any two of the following: John of Gaunt; the Bishop of Carlisle; Northumberland. (London University, G.C.E., Ordinary Level, Autumn 1956.)

These two questions have been chosen as examples here because, although each asks for a detailed knowledge of the character, and the part taken in the play, by John of Gaunt, each requires a rather different selection and handling of material.

Make some *brief notes* before you begin to write. Remember that you will certainly not have time to write out the whole essay in rough and then copy it out later. Plan carefully: the way in which the question is arranged will tell you how to plan your answer.

Any *quotations* given should be short; do not waste time on long quotations of ten or twenty lines; it is more important to show that you yourself can write simply and clearly. When quoting poetry, quote in lines and begin the quotation about one inch from the left-hand margin. The quotations given should fit grammatically into your own sentences.

QUESTION 3

Plan: Plan to give two thirds of your time to the *part taken.* John of Gaunt will need rather less than half of this (because he dies early in the play) and the Duke of York will need rather more. Divide the rest of your time evenly between *similarities* and *differences.* These, then, will be the four paragraphs of your answer: part taken by John of Gaunt; part taken by York; similarities; differences.

Material: from all the scenes where these two characters appear, but especially those in which they appear with their nephew Richard.

Arrangement: Begin the first paragraph at once, without an introduction; you earn marks only for information given, e.g.

> The Duke of Lancaster believes that he should be loyal to the king even if the king has done wrong; he tells the Duchess of Gloucester that he cannot "lift an angry arm" against God's deputy, even if Richard was responsible for Gloucester's murder.

Keep to one tense, either past or present, throughout your essay.

Finish the *part taken* by Gaunt in four or five good sentences:

> G. gives his vote for the banishment of Bolingbroke (why? What does he put first, his own wishes or the good of the country?). As he dies, speaks with sorrow of Richard's extravagance and weakness (Do we believe him?). R., he thinks, is acting so foolishly that he will depose himself. (How does this turn out to be true? What particularly foolish thing does R. do, after Gaunt's death?)

Remember that *part taken* means "in the structure of the play".

In the *second paragraph* you have much to say in a short space. Begin at once and make your points briefly. Do not be led away into telling a great piece of the story in any detail.

> York points out to Richard that in taking Bolingbroke's inheritance he will unite against himself all the English nobles; he wants justice for Bolingbroke.
>
> "Was not Gaunt just, and is not Harry true?"

Finish this paragraph in five or six good sentences:

> Y. cannot get together money and men to oppose Bolingbroke; finally he is won over (by what?) and agrees to go with Bolingbroke to (where?). It is Y. who brings to Parliament the news that R. is ready to give up his crown; he then transfers his loyalty to the next king, Henry IV. One last sentence about the Aumerle plot, telling what it shows about York's feelings for the new king.

The *third paragraph* on similarities should begin with a simple sentence to show that you have now reached this part of the answer.

> Gaunt and York are similar in that they are both (loyal to the crown, they put personal considerations second). They both want to see England (Name two or three things they want for their country).

Do not repeat here the information given in paragraphs one and two, but refer to it, e.g. they put second their love for their sons.

For *paragraph four* be content to make two points only, and make them very simply. You will not have time for more. Begin the paragraph with a few words to show where you have got to in your essay: e.g.

> They are different in that Gaunt seems very fond of his son, while York seems (what? I have written *seems* not *is*, because I have to judge by what the two men say and perhaps, in fact, York loved Aumerle as much as Gaunt loved Bolingbroke). Your second point could be that Gaunt is less respectful to the king (when? Give one line of quotation from this scene). York has more personal sympathy for Richard. (Give an example from where he describes how

Richard came riding into London and how he was received. One line of quotation would make the point very shortly.)

The essay ends here; you will have no need, and no time, for a conclusion.

QUESTION 4

Plan: You will probably choose John of Gaunt and Northumberland, as these will give you most material. Give half your time to each character, writing one long paragraph for each.

Remember to refer to *speeches and actions*, but do not try to have a separate paragraph for each of these sections. What each man *says* and *does* will go together in one paragraph. Note that you are not asked *in this question* (although you might be in other questions) what the other characters in the play have to say about these two men.

This question is different from Question 3; for a *character-sketch* you must say what a man is like as a person, and not so much what he causes to happen in the play.

Material and Arrangement: The arrangement here is much easier than for Question 3, because you can take the actions and speeches in the order in which they come in the play. But you must be careful to word your sentences so that each action or speech to which you refer serves as an example to show something of the man's character.

Begin at once, without introduction, with the beginning of the play; you have much to say in a short space. Do not be trapped into telling the story; each sentence must be about the character you have chosen, e.g.:

> John of Gaunt is very proud of his family name. We see that, although he is very fond of his son Bolingbroke, he does not try to hold him back from his fight with Mowbray. He tries to comfort him as he goes into banishment:
>
> Go, say I sent thee forth to purchase honour
> And not the king exiled thee.

You will have time for about five or six other points, very briefly made, e.g.

> loyal to the king; seems to his sister-in-law to be too (what? Supply two adjectives) . . . because he will not . . . to avenge (what?)
> old and weak, worried about the state of England and about Richard's . . . and . . . (Supply two or three nouns here, and perhaps one line of quotation)
> tactless in his rebuke of (whom? What does he say?). Jokes bitterly about (what?)

Begin your second paragraph with the name of the character you have chosen, and, perhaps, a short sentence of comment, e.g.

> Northumberland is a less sympathetic character. He and some of the other nobles are ready to support Bolingbroke (why? self-interest, to save their own property, to gain the favour of man whose power may become very great; or, desire for justice?). Active and efficient, meets B. (say when and where in six or seven words) and rides with him to (give place and purpose, in four words). Flatters B. saying (quote a few words). At Bristol is put in charge of (eight or ten words). When he brings the message of Bolingbroke to Richard at Flint Castle, he does not (what action does he omit?), but he carries the messages correctly. In the Parliament Hall, he tries to insist that (What does he want R. to do? Quote one line, if possible). Is present at Richard's parting from his queen, and seems (What feelings does he show?) R. foretells that N. will want from Bolingbroke, as a reward for (what?) more than (what?). In the whole play is anything shown of his nobility of character?